Apologetics and the Eclipse of Mystery

Apologetics
and the Eclipse of Mystery

MYSTAGOGY ACCORDING TO
KARL RAHNER

James J. Bacik

UNIVERSITY OF NOTRE DAME PRESS

NOTRE DAME   LONDON

Library of Congress Cataloging in Publication Data

Bacik, James J   1936–
  Apologetics and the eclipse of mystery.

  Bibliography: p.
  Includes index.
  1. Apologetics—20th century. 2. Mystery.
3. Rahner, Karl, 1904– I. Title.
BT1102.B2   230   80-123
ISBN 0-268-00592-3

Manufactured in the United States of America

Contents

Introduction, by Karl Rahner   ix

Foreword, by John Macquarrie   xi

Author's Preface   xiii

PART ONE

1. The Eclipse of Mystery   3

2. In Search of Mystery   12

3. The Experience of Mystery   20

4. Disclosing Mystery   39

5. Mystagogy Defended   48

PART TWO

6. Models of Mystery Explained   65

7. Models of Mystery   75

8. Mystery Vindicated   104

Notes   127

Bibliography   143

Name Index   161

Subject Index   164

Introduction

NATURALLY A THEOLOGIAN feels honored and pleased when some-
body writes about his theology. For the theologian works in the
service both of God's revelation and of the Church and therefore
desires that his books should be read. He feels himself even more
honored and pleased when another helps him in that task. This is
the case with this book by James J. Bacik—originally a doctoral thesis
at the University of Oxford which received high praise from Dr.
John Macquarrie, the supervisor, and the readers Dr. Edward Yar-
nold and Dr. Hugo Meynell. Even though there are many books
about my theology, it is my opinion that this one is particularly
notable because it deals with a concept (mystagogy) which on the one
hand gives access to much of my theology and on the other has not
been so fully developed by myself that it precludes another book on
the topic. Whether or not all the goals of this book have been attained I leave to the judgment of the aforementioned theologians
whose opinions I gladly respect. However, the treatment of the concept of mystagogy remains important both in itself and for my theology because of the close connection between fundamental and dogmatic theology and between theory and practice. It is in the light of
these relationships that the centrality of this concept in my theology
is to be seen.

I would like to take this opportunity to say a few words about
the relationship between my theology and the political theology
(practische Fundamentaltheologie) of J.B. Metz, my student and friend.
In his latest book *Glaube in Geschichte und Gesellschaft,* (Mainz, 1977;
English trans.: *Faith in History and Society,* Seabury, 1979) Metz insists
on going beyond my own theology to a societal situation of man and
the Christian praxis, precisely because this praxis is not merely the
carrying out of an abstract Christian theory. Metz's critique of my
theology (which he calls transcendental theology) is the only criticism
which I take very seriously. I agree in general with the positive

contribution in Metz's book. Insofar as the critique by Metz is correct, every concrete mystagogy must obviously from the very beginning consider the societal situation and the Christian praxis to which it addresses itself. If this is not sufficiently done in my theory of mystagogy and in its explanation in this book, then this theory must be filled out. However it is not therefore false. For it has always been clear in my theology that a "transcendental experience" (of God and of grace) is always mediated through a categorical experience in history, in interpersonal relationships, and in society. If one not only sees and takes seriously these necessary mediations of transcendental experience but also fills it out in a concrete way, then one already practices in an authentic way political theology, or, in other words, a practical fundamental theology. On the other hand, such a political theology is, if it truly wishes to concern itself with God, not possible without reflection on those essential characteristics of man which a transcendental theology discloses. Therefore, I believe that my theology and that of Metz are not necessarily contradictory. However, I gladly recognize that a concrete mystagogy must, to use Metz's language, be at the same time "mystical and political." It would be good if the reader of Fr. Bacik's book would not forget this point. Even if it does not expressly thematize this aspect of an adequate mystagogy (since nobody can say everything at once), this book is significant and important since it treats a theme which is of fundamental significance for pastoral work in a secularized world. Therefore I genuinely extend my gratitude to James Bacik for writing it.

Karl Rahner, S.J.

München, Advent 1977

Foreword

ONE OFTEN HEARS the complaint today that there is a gulf between the Church's theologians and the ordinary believers or even the parish clergy. There may be some truth in this, for every subject nowadays, theology included, seems to become increasingly specialized, and only those who have been trained in its language and methods and who are able to find time to read the constant flow of new literature can hope to keep fully abreast of its development. Yet theology exists to serve the Church and to sift and clarify its teachings. It has no life of its own apart from the faith which it seeks to interpret. Thus even if it is necessary for the theologian sometimes to use unfamiliar terminology and to engage in discussions that seem far removed from the life of the ordinary Christian congregation, he will not and must not forget his relation to the life of the Church, and his obligation to strengthen that life.

It must be counted one of the blessings of our time that the most eminent Catholic theologian in the period of change inaugurated by Vatican II, Dr. Karl Rahner, is one in whose theology a strong pastoral interest has always been apparent. It is impossible to read him without sensing his deep concern for the faith, the Church, indeed, the whole human race as made in God's image and the recipients of his self-communication. All this shines through his work, though it has also to be said that much of his language is very difficult and discourages even readers with a theological training.

Perhaps the most important area of Dr. Rahner's pastoral concern is his reaching out to those on the fringes of the Church or beyond the fringes—the many men and women of our time who have a deep moral integrity and a social responsibility but who are held back in a secular age by various difficulties that prevent them from identifying with the Christian faith. In approaching such persons with full respect for their intellectual integrity Dr. Rahner in many ways has made use of the concept of mystery. Even amidst the brilliant achievements of modern science—perhaps *especially* amidst them—we become aware of a hidden depth that is not exhausted by our empirical studies. That depth is there first of all in human existence itself, but reflection upon it leads us to the ultimate mystery of God.

There is no question about Dr. Rahner's pastoral concern, but, as already hinted, he is no popular theologian and his writings are difficult. In Dr. James Bacik he has found a brilliant interpreter. Dr. Bacik has closely studied the Rahnerian corpus for years and has not only mastered the intricate thoughts contained in these writings but has put them together and interpreted them with a clarity which will touch a wider readership than the original. But this is not simply interpretation, for there is also creativity in Dr. Bacik's work as he applies deep theological insights to the pastoral tasks in which he has been engaged for many years. His book is at once an illuminating introduction to one of the great theologians of our century and a major resource to all who are seeking to commend the Christian faith today.

John Macquarrie

University of Oxford
June, 1979

Preface

THIS BOOK, I BELIEVE, can be read profitably from at least three different perspectives. It is, first of all, intended as an aid for those who are engaged in the apologetic effort to make the Christian faith intelligible and credible to our contemporaries. As such, it begins with the premise that a significant number of people in the Western World today are impoverished by a diminished or distorted sense of the mysterious depths of human existence (Chapter One). In this situation it is not sufficient simply to interpret and refocus Christian doctrines. Rather, the apologist must first of all attend to the often neglected task of disclosing and articulating the mystery dimension implicit in all human experience so that Christian doctrines can be related to genuine human concerns (Chapter Two). This mystery dimension can be uncovered by looking more closely at our self-experience, which includes gradations of conscious awareness moving from a vague mood to a carefully articulated self-awareness. With this understanding of human consciousness, it is possible to show that all of our self-experience has a necessary relation to an encompassing mystery which is both the source and goal of our human activity. This analysis lays the foundation for the claim that religious experience is not confined to one area of our lives, but is the essential, if often eclipsed, depth dimension of all our experience (Chapter Three). In order to bring this religious experience to conscious awareness, the apologist can tap the insights of the humanistic sciences, make use of careful and vivid descriptions of human experience, employ various meditation techniques, and utilize the capacity of theology to point beyond itself to the absolute mystery (Chapter Four). After a defense of this theoretical framework for the first step in a contemporary apologetics (Chapter Five), I offer in the second part of the book two 'models of mystery' which are designed to disclose the depth dimension in specific areas of our experience. The models are dependent on insights from Rahner and possess similiarities to material presented by other authors, especially Langdon Gilkey's prolegomena to theology in *Naming the Whirlwind*. However, I believe these models have something distinct to offer, especially because they root a phenomenology of common human experience in universal structures of human existence suggested by a theological anthoropology (Chapter Six). The first model examines human questioning and roots it in the unfulfilled dynamism of the human spirit, whch tends toward absolute mystery. The second model describes human freedom and love, showing how they are grounded in the acceptance of self as essentially dependent on the absolute good (Chapter Seven). Finally, since it is not sufficient merely to describe the mystery dimension in human life without offering any proof of its actual existence, I have summarized both direct (metaphysical) and indirect vindications of the claim that our spiritual activities necessarily imply the existence of the absolute mystery as a condition of their possibility (Chapter Eight).

It will be helpful to keep in mind the progressive character of the argumentation, to realize that important assumptions are clarified and vindicated only in the last chapter, and to note that this book is not a complete defense of the Christian faith but concentrates on the often neglected first step which is necessary for an effective contemporary apologetics. Thus, by disclosing and articulating the mystery dimension of our common human experience, this book sets the stage for the traditional apologetic task of explaining and vindicating belief in the God of the Bible and in Jesus of Nazareth as the absolute savior.

The second perspective from which the book can be read is as an interpretation and application of the thought of the great German Jesuit theologian Karl Rahner. In looking for help in dealing with the eclipse of mystery, I turned to Rahner's notion of 'mystagogy.' He borrowed the term from classical liturgical writings, where it refers to initiation into the sacramental life of the Church, and applied it to the effort to initiate people today into a sense of mystery as the foundation for an authentic appropriation of Christian doctrines. Thus the mystagogical task is to enable persons to interpret correctly their deeper experiences, to move from a vague awareness of the mystery dimension of their lives to a greater conceptual clarity, to find a proper symbolization of their genuine religious experience. Although Rahner has not fully developed this notion of mystagogy, it is central to his whole theology, as he himself admits in the Introduction to this book. If we read Rahner using mystagogy as an interpretive key, then we are more likely to notice that religious experience has been the basis for his theological reflection from his very first articles up to the most recent ones. It becomes clear that he developed a radically anthropocentric approach in his early work and has employed it increasingly in his later writings. We will also recognize that his theological anthropology, which insists that all human beings are essentially oriented to mystery, functions as a powerful searchlight which he uses to illume all problems presented to him by the modern world. Finally, when reading him from this viewpoint of mystagogy, it becomes obvious that genuine pastoral concerns have indeed dominated all of his theological writings.

There seems to be a feeling in some circles that Rahmer's day has passed. Some contend that he was a brilliant and constructive reinterpreter of traditional scholastic theology but that the need for this work in now over. Others see him merely as a subtle defender of traditional Church teaching. I hope that my effort in this book to highlight his interest in religious experience, to employ his theological anthropology in responding to the contemporary eclipse of mystery, and to develop his seminal ideas on mystagogy will clearly demonstrate the continuing significance of Rahner's work. He has indeed played an important role in the past as a reinterpreter of scholasticism and traditional doctrine. However, I see his value for the days ahead in the fact that he is a perceptive Christian interpreter of common human experience who provides us with a comprehensive theological framework as well as penetrating insights into the contemporary situation.

Readers with a special interest in Rahner should pay close attention to Chapter Five where his ideas, which are employed throughout the book, are discussed explicitly. The bibliography, which is a rather comprehensive listing of Rahner's works available in both German and English as of 1978, should prove valuable. In using the footnotes which identify Rahner's works, it will be useful to remember these points: in commonly cited works, his name as the author is often omitted; the article titles are abbreviated; *TI* stands for *Theological Investigations,* ST for *Schriften Theologie,* SW for *Spirit in the World,* and *GW* for *Geist in Welt;* the abbreviations of the book titles (this is true for other authors as well) are found in the bibliography; the original German is noted in parentheses. In many cases the critical apparatus employed in the original version of this book (numerous footnotes, technical discussions, original German texts, etc.) has been deleted in the interest of brevity. I hope this does not detract from an appreciation of the depth and subtlety of Rahner's insights.

Thirdly, the book can be read for personal enrichment even by those with no direct interest in apologetics or Rahnerian theology. Persons reading from this perspective might find it helpful to be on alert for the development of the following points. There are a variety of ways in which we can suffer from a diminished or distorted sense of mystery. We need to cultivate an awareness of our deeper experiences and learn how to relate Christian doctrines to our real life concerns. Genuine religious experience is really available to all of us and not just a privileged few. There is a depth dimension in even our ordinary experience, and the recognition of this can help us deal both with a culture which celebrates the superficial and also with current religious groups which seem to overemphasize the extraordinary and spectacular types of religious experience. It is possible for us to uncover the mysterious depths of our self-experience through meditation involving confrontation with our true self. The fact that our questioning never finds totally satisfying answers and that we call our life as a whole into question shows that we are essentially oriented to an infinite mystery. When we reflect on the best of our human relationships, we realize that love possesses a mysterious dynamism which promotes the individuality of the beloved and at the same time directs us toward the absolute good which alone can satisfy our longings.

By looking for elaborations of these propositions in the text, you may find that material which seems abstract can be made more concrete and personal. Those reading only from this perspective may find it better to skip the more technical material in Chapters Five and Eight.

I am grateful to Fr. Rahner for the considerable time he spent discussing and advising me on this project and also for writing the Introduction upon its completion. Despite the brilliance of his thought and the power of his personality, I realize that the proper response to Rahner is not strict discipleship but an effort to reflect creatively on the contemporary situation in the light of the Christian tradition.

My gratitude also goes to Dr. John Macquarrie, who directed this project in its original form as a doctoral thesis at Oxford. His great breadth of scholarship and fine human sensitivity are impressive to me, and I appreciate the Foreword he contributed. Rather than attempt to list all the other people who have assisted me in completing this book, I will simply make a general acknowledgement of my great debt of gratitude to a number of very generous friends.

PART ONE

CHAPTER ONE

The Eclipse of Mystery

THE CHRISTIAN APOLOGIST must always address real people in their historically and culturally conditioned situation. If the Christian message is to be communicated effectively in the years ahead, it is important to be in touch with the various self-understandings available in our culture and to recognize the factors that shape our consciousness and motivate our behavior.

I. THEOLOGICAL PERSPECTIVE

Theology could perform a valuable service by gathering insights into the contemporary consciousness from various sources and placing them in a religious framework. This is a difficult task precisely because of the accelerating change which dominates our era and because in a transition period it is difficult to delineate clearly the features of the new consciousness. While there are certain elements which remain the same (people continue to question, to love, to suffer loneliness, to demand happiness and to face death), the rapidly changing cultural situation makes it difficult to discern the precise coloration of even these primary experiences. In addition, it is true that we find a variety of self-understandings available even in a particular geographical area such as the United States, so that we cannot speak simply about contemporary consciousness or modern man.

With these points in mind I want to isolate one particular problem faced by Christian apologists in dealing with many of their contemporaries: the eclipse of a proper sense of mystery. This is an umbrella phrase which indicates that a sizable number of people in the modern Western world have a diminished or distorted perception of the deeper dimensions of their experience—the mysterious depths that are necessarily present even though temporarily hidden

3

or misunderstood. This general problem is experienced by people today in various forms and is best understood by examining its particular manifestations. Therefore, keeping in mind the limitations and dangers of stereotyping, let us analyze five types of individuals who suffer from the diminishments and distortions of the eclipse of mystery.

1. Secularized Atheists

There is no doubt that the Christian apologist must respond to the fact that the modern world has produced a new and distinctive secular self-understanding. In discussing this phenomenon it became fashionable to speak of "secular man" in an uncritical way, identifying him as an atheist and predicting that soon everyone will share his outlook. A more accurate picture emerges when secularization is viewed as a limited process in which particular regions of human activity gradually achieve a greater autonomy and are less dependent on the authority of the Church as a social entity.[1] Thus, the world is separating itself from the Church and not necessarily from God, which means that secularization need not be interpreted as a totally antireligious process. In addition, it is an evolving process which indicates that its effects are not yet universal and that people are touched by it in various ways.

It must be emphasized that secularization is a fundamentally ambivalent process.[2] On the one hand, it is a legitimate development of a Christian outlook which grants the world its proper autonomy and calls upon human beings to shape it. The world is not a god, nor a static reality directly controlled by God, but the proper sphere for our creative activity. The growing autonomy of the world is therefore a legitimate development which is based ultimately on the fact that it is a creation of God placed at our disposal. This positive evaluation remains true even though historically the Church has fought against such autonomy, and despite the fact that the actual separation of the secular world from the influence of the Church has often been marked by bitterness and strife.

On the other hand, the secularization process, legitimate in itself, carries the danger of an atheistic interpretation. It can be regarded as a total explanation of the whole human existence. It can give rise to a secular humanism which is passionate about social change and the betterment of mankind but which has no sense of the mystery dimension of life. As a matter of fact, in our world come of age a special form of atheism has arisen which results precisely

from the fact that we have achieved a greater ability to control ourselves and the world. Secularized atheists find no room for God as
they engage in various areas of human activity which are now removed from the authority of the Church.

In trying to specify the causes of secularized atheism, we can
begin with the rationalism engendered by the natural sciences.
These sciences employ a methodology which attempts to explain all
phenomena in terms of functional connections, and which refuses to
invoke an intervention of God to explain currently inexplicable
phenomena. The atheist simply takes this scientific mentality and
gives it universal application making it a comprehensive outlook on
life as a whole. It is not so much that God's existence is positively
denied, but rather that God simply does not enter the picture or
make any practical difference. In other words, the religious language of transcendence and mystery is judged to be simply meaningless. Hence the precise problem today is not nineteenth-century
scientism which thought it knew for certain that there was no God.
While we find remnants of this view, the secularized atheist lacks
such dogmatic certitude. Nor is the problem that science has or will
discover some clear and certain piece of information against which
Christian faith must protest. The difficulty is not even in the goal of
science to understand reality in a unified and functional way. Such
an interpretation can coexist with a faith perspective in the same
person. The problem comes only when the scientific mentality attempts to become a comprehensive view of the whole of human
existence, thus effectively eclipsing mystery and excluding God.

The growing ability to control the world and to manipulate
human existence is a related but distinct cause of secularized atheism.[3] We no longer simply live in a predetermined environment but
now face the exhilarating, if frightening, task of creating and shaping the world. Even more importantly, we have begun to engineer
our own nature through genetic, psychological, and sociological
means, and we sense that this trend will continue to grow. Some
people become so taken with this ability and its attendant responsibilities that they are inclined to judge any talk of God as rather
childish and unimportant in comparison. For them man becomes the
measure of man, and the language of mystery becomes meaningless.
They are so fascinated by the capabilities of technology that they
begin to understand themselves on the model of a sophisticated
computer. In short, the ability to shape the world and themselves
leads to an atheistic self-interpretation.

The Christian apologist must deal with people who are touched by this ambivalent process of secularization, including those who are not explicitly aware of it or its influence. While some individuals fruitfully combine a positive perception of the autonomy of the world with a comprehensive theistic interpretation of their own existence, others take on a secularized consciousness in which data and logical deduction exhaust their conscious perceptions of reality. They are immersed in a secular mood dominated by a desire for autonomy and possessed of little sense of the need to submit to a higher power. They do not consciously understand themselves as dependent on an ultimate source or moving toward a transcendent goal. In short, for them the mystery dimension of life is eclipsed, and an effective apologetics must first deal with this problem.

2. Skeptics

The complexity of our modern world has produced a growing number of skeptics who refuse to make explicit judgments and commitments about the deepest questions of life, including the existence of God. They believe that this reserve is for them the only intellectually honest response to the modern knowledge explosion and the fact of accelerating change. Mystery is eclipsed for them in the sense that its gracious character is obscured and the potential richness of a personal commitment effectively hidden.

The skeptics bring to focus important elements in our world today. It is true the sum total of human experience and knowledge has become so vast and complex that no science or intellectual discipline can systematize or integrate it. We do have to contend with a bewildering array of competing world views and philosophies. It seems that even the Christian faith can no longer synthesize all other aspects of life nor achieve the status of a totally comprehensive system.[4] In a previous age Christianity could perform this function because it held together a homogeneous culture and provided a social matrix in which a comprehensive and integrating religious outlook was simply taken for granted. With the death of Christendom this structure collapses, Christians are in a minority position, the culture is shaped by other forces, and a pluralism of world views becomes available. This objective situation makes it increasingly difficult for individuals to achieve a satisfying intellectual synthesis of their own. Some people are very aware of their inability to integrate completely their own experience, to reduce their own knowledge to a comprehensive system, to understand the available insights of others. They realize that the culture no longer supplies a clear-cut, unified answer to the problems of human existence, and the task of working out a viable position of one's own is taxing and subject to error. Given this situation, the skeptic fails to achieve a satisfying intellectual synthesis and refuses any ultimate commitments.

In our pluralistic culture where the knowledge explosion is accelerating, the Christian apologist is bound to encounter a growing number of people who tend toward such a skeptical position: they are doubtful about the mysterious forces in their lives and afraid to commit themselves to the position that the mystery which envelops them is absolute and trustworthy.

3. The Troubled Atheist

The apologist today encounters a significant number of people who, due to a sharpened sense of the evils of life, find it increasingly difficult to affirm the existence of a good God. This perception of evil—whether very personal (the heaviness of life, the loss of meaning and purpose, the pettiness of everyday existence, etc.) or more public (the cruelty of history, mass starvation, wars, etc.)—makes it difficult to believe that existence is gracious, that the mystery in control of the world is benign. For them it is the friendly countenance of mystery which is overshadowed.

Of course, all people encounter evil in their lives, but some seem more inclined to brush it off or block it out. In many ways our culture tends to reinforce this tendency by giving the impression that all is well, happiness is just around the corner, problems can be solved by taking pills or changing the channel, and joy is cheap and easy. Society offers many means for avoiding the frightening business of facing the dark side of life: compulsive work, escapist entertainment, refined pleasures, and the like.

However, there are those who refuse these escapes and allow themselves to be touched deeply by evil. They thus experience the absence of a friendly deity or the eclipse of gracious mystery and are moved to judge human existence as absurd. We are reminded here of strains of modern existentialism and of Camus' notion of the absurd hero as the one who accepts this situation nobly and uncompromisingly.[5] While the Christian apologist will encounter a limited number of Sisyphean heroes, there are many more who find their beliefs challenged and their capacity for constructive action diminished by their encounters with the darkness of evil.

4. The Silent Believers

There are people today who are so impressed by the all-embracing mystery of life that they are suspicious of any attempt to express or objectify it in dogmas, theological systems, or ritual. They view these various objectifications as either childish or crude attempts to manipulate the essentially mysterious character of existence and regard their own silence in the face of mystery as purer and more noble than the naive belief systems which attempt to particularize it. While these people often appear to be atheistic at an explicit level, they are clearly not rationalists or positivists. On the contrary, they have a deep, if silent, reverence for mystery. However, the silent believers are in danger of finding mystery effectively eclipsed since it is incapable of shining through any of the particularities of this world.

This position can result, on the one hand, from a pronounced sense of the greatness and vastness of the mystery, so that a person feels that it is irreverent to speak about it. There is such a great distance between religious expression and the reality it signifies that it is better to remain silent. It can, on the other hand, involve a devaluing of the historical, material, concrete character of existence. This disdain for the particularity of human life makes it difficult to accept the fact that the transcendent deity manifests itself in the ordinary things of this world. In any case there is a "scandal of particularity" which affects a number of our contemporaries, causing them to restrict mystery to a zone of silence. They are reluctant to speak glibly about their deepest experiences of life and are uncomfortable in the presence of those who do. This reaction carries over into a distrust of institutional religion because it appears to trivialize the most significant aspects of their experience. Since they have encountered no religious articulations that ring true to them, they often adopt an atheistic interpretation of life, and consider themselves to have achieved a more refined outlook than their theistic friends. However, the apologist will do better to approach them as silent believers and to attempt to understand their reluctance to speak about religious matters. The real task is to provide an acceptable justification for all of the various objectifications (doctrines, liturgy, scriptures, etc.) as legitimate and helpful pointers to the transcendent mystery.

5. Pipeline Believers

The general problem of an eclipse of mystery finds still another manifestation among some fervent dogmatic believers (we might think here of tendencies within the contemporary pentecostal and charismatic renewal) who seem to claim a pipeline to God, a direct and immediate revelation from the deity. Thus, individuals speak of direct manifestations of God's will, of an exclusive possession of God's truth, of an unambiguous understanding of the biblical message, of clear predictions of the future. There is a danger here of a new form of the heresy of ontologism[6] which ends up denying that the divine mystery is received according to our own capacities and is mediated to us through the finite created world. When this occurs, the authentic understanding of mystery as being essentially incomprehensible is lost and is replaced by a controlling, manipulating and demanding attitude. Mystery is eclipsed by being reduced to manageable proportions. Furthermore, when an ontologistic outlook becomes prevalent, people who have never had striking religious experiences can adversely be affected. They may feel inadequate and guilty, or be moved to a frantic search for such experiences, or be inclined toward atheistic interpretations of their own limited experience.

In dealing with those tending toward ontologism the apologist encounters a subtle destruction of mystery which tends to reduce it to merely human proportions while the language of transcendence is maintained.

II. SECULAR PERSPECTIVE

The preceding theological analysis, which suggests that many people in our culture suffer from a diminished or distorted sense of mystery, finds support from secular sources as well. For example, Elisabeth Kübler-Ross has brought to popular attention the fact that the mystery of death has been thoroughly repressed in the United States.[7] We live in a culture where among many death is still a taboo topic. Even when it is discussed, it is often in terms of a problem to be solved (for instance, how to freeze bodies for later resuscitation) rather than a mystery encountered. Karl Menninger, working out of his experiences as a psychotherapist, has reminded us that many suffer from a vague guilt and anxiety precisely because in our society the mystery of sin and responsibility has been denied.[8] When the word 'sin' falls out of our operative vocabulary, we have no language with which to deal with the mysterious depths of our being where we know that we are ultimately responsible for ourselves. The economist Robert Heilbroner has given us a powerful critique of a culture dominated by science and technology and affected with a vague sense of hopelessness and "an oppressive anticipation of the future."[9] Our confidence is shaken because external events seem beyond our control, and we are not able to pass on our deepest values to the next generation. We are forced to face the fact that reason has its limits in dealing with our social problems. There is also a "civilizational malaise" which results from the inability of material satisfactions to satisfy the mysterious longings of the human spirit for meaning and purpose.

Even Marxist-inspired critiques remind us of the eclipse of mystery. Herbert Marcuse claims that our society produces "one-dimensional" individuals who have lost the ability to imagine qualitatively better alternatives and the power to transcend the limitations of the culture.[10] Life becomes flat and dull, and the human spirit is imprisoned within the established order. This critique helps us to understand the power of a "one-dimensional society" to level the human spirit. Social and economic structures possess a surprising capacity to co-opt individual initiative and creativity. Technology becomes an idol and functions as a dehumanizing force. From this viewpoint the eclipse of mystery is not just a private problem for the individual but a societal malaise that impoverishes the whole culture. In this situation it is difficult for a person to rise above the cultural norm and to achieve an adequate understanding of the deepest aspects of human experience. Atheism takes on a public character and an air of respectability. The language becomes restricted, and we have no way of speaking about the mysterious depths of our existence. This analysis reminds apologists of the extent and difficulty of their task and suggests that radical responses are called for.

III. HISTORICAL PERSPECTIVE

In taking seriously the problem of the eclipse of mystery the contemporary apologist builds on important thinkers who have attempted to respond to the realities of the modern world. For example, we can recall Friedrich Schleiermacher, who in 1799, sensing that the mysterious dimension of human experience had to be rediscovered, told the "cultured despisers of religion": "I would conduct you into the profoundest depths whence every feeling and conception receives its form. I would show you from what human tendency religion proceeds and how it belongs to what is for you

highest and dearest."[11] In our own century Rudolf Otto understood the problem in a similar way, which he expressed in terms of
the need to elicit an often hidden sense of the numinous or divine:

> There is only one way to help another to an understanding of
> it. He must be guided and led on by consideration and discus-
> sion of the matter through the ways of his own mind, until he
> reach the point at which 'the numinous' in him perforce begins
> to stir, to start into life and into consciousness.[12]

Today Karl Rahner continues to enunciate this theme under the
heading of the need for a modern mystagogy:

> Theological science itself has not yet tackled even in theory the
> phenomenon of a worldwide atheism that appears self-evident
> to itself. We do not yet possess a mystagogy in the experience
> of God and his grace which would be practicable for the ordi-
> nary pastor and which would appeal to our sceptical, scientifi-
> cally trained contemporaries.[13]

He understands that the modern pluralistic world has helped produce a skeptical or atheistic attitude and that a pastoral response is
needed which counters this tendency by first initiating people into a
conscious awareness of their deeper experience of life. In our terms
it is a question of an eclipse of mystery which calls for a nuanced
response from the Christian apologist.

CHAPTER TWO

In Search of Mystery

WHEN DEALING WITH people who have a diminished or distorted sense of mystery, how is the Christian apologist to proceed? In this chapter we will begin our response by developing a twofold approach based on Karl Rahner's very helpful suggestions for a modern mystagogy.[1]

I. CATEGORICAL MYSTAGOGY

For those who find the mystery dimension of life obscured, Christian doctrines tend to appear as abstract speculations divorced from any experiential base. Their proper function of pointing to the mysterious depths of the divine-human relationship is lost amidst literalistic interpretations. In this situation the Christian apologist must find a convincing method of relating experience and Christian doctrine. Here we will discuss this problem under the heading of "categorical mystagogy."[2]

1. An effective apologetics must flow from a sound theological methodology. Rahner provides us with some helpful suggestions along this line. A contemporary theology must bring the *fides quae*, or content of faith, into a close and explicitly recognized unity with the *fides qua*, or the very act of faith itself.[3] The point is that theology must discuss and express individual doctrines with constant attention to the interests, needs, and capabilities of the inquirer. It is a question not merely of determining how to present effectively a fixed set of doctrines but of doing theology while maintaining an active empathy for the struggle to make faith a reality. Theologians do not have to be culpable doubters, but their work must reflect their own involvement in the modern crisis of faith. Not only is this true for the Christian tradition as a whole in relation to a general act of faith, but it applies also to formulating individual doctrines with a view to

the very specific problem of accepting and assimilating that particular teaching. In short, content and subjective disposition must be consciously unified.

This goal is facilitated by an anthropocentric approach in which the theologian carefully examines the structures of human consciousness which make the appropriation of particular Christian truths possible.[4] What is the subjective horizon of understanding within which a dogma can be made intelligible? What aspects of common self-understanding already correspond to the content of Christian teaching? What human experiences provide a perspective for sensing the importance of the redemptive actions of Jesus, for example? An apologetically effective theology must take these kinds of questions seriously and attempt to work out more precise answers.

Standing behind this theological methodology is the conviction that human experience and Christian doctrines are connected not simply logically and externally but organically and intrinsically.[5] Thus, because our concrete personal existence is graced, there is an intrinsic ontological connection between our self-experience and the content of particular doctrines. It is not a matter of uniting disparate realities by verbal or logical methods. Rather, experience and doctrine grow out of a common graced matrix. They must be intrinsically connected because of their common origin. Here is the key to understanding the mystagogical task of relating experience and doctrine. It is not a clever technique for making doctrines intelligible, but an elucidation of common meanings found both in our experience and also in Christian doctrines which are actually objectifications of graced human experience. In other words, revealed doctrine is not apart from, or outside, human experience but is the verbalized precipitate of that experience. On this premise one expects to find organic connections between doctrine and experience. An anthropocentric theology will attempt to uncover and employ these links and in doing so will perform a mystagogical function. For example, we could do a phenomenology of human longings to show that our deepest desire is for an absolute meaning and final validity for our life. Once this common human experience was articulated, we would be in a position to understand the Resurrection of Jesus, not as a totally strange or foreign miracle, but as the guarantee that there is an ultimate fulfillment for our desires.

2. Perhaps we can highlight the apologetic potential of Rahner's approach by comparing it with Paul Tillich's "method of correlation."[6] Tillich, while using different terminology, shares Rahner's fundamental interests. Tillich speaks of message and situa-

tion rather than experience and doctrine, and he wants to relate them so that neither of them is destroyed. He insists that Christian answers cannot be deduced from the situation itself, but must nevertheless respond to questions flowing from the situation as interpreted by man. And finally he advises, as does Rahner, that the theologian can offer convincing answers only if he has shared the human predicament and struggled for the answers.

The difference comes to light when we ask precisely how situation and message are related. Tillich says they are correlated, which means that they are two independent elements which are interdependent. Thus he can write: "The existential question, namely, man himself in the conflicts of his existential situation, is not the source for the revelatory answer formulated by theology."[7] In other words, the situation produces no answers, only questions.[8] Natural theology can analyze the human situation, but can offer no theological affirmation because God is manifest only through himself. Thus situation and message for Tillich are correlated as question and answer, and any search for the organic connections described above is theoretically ruled out. The situation questions; it does not disclose. The fundamental reason for Tillich's position, it seems to me, is that he does not appreciate the graced character of both the situation and our interpretation of it. On the contrary, Rahner has come to see clearly that we live in one graced world. This fact establishes a fundamental organic unity between experience and doctrine, allows believers to value the answers derived from human culture, and permits them to accept doctrine, not as an external message, but as an objective articulation of human experience which is always already affected by grace. Hence Rahner can write:

> The secular world, as secular, has an inner mysterious depth, in all its earthly mysteries from birth to death, through which, by the grace of God, it is open to God and his infinitely incomprehensible love even when it is not, before receiving the explicit message of the gospel, aware of it. Not only are there many anonymous Christians; there is also an anonymously Christian world. For whenever its demands and its reality are really met and endured in the whole breadth and depth of natural human existence and in the totality of human life, then, according to Christian teachings, the grace of Christ is already at work and this response and endurance are already something Christian, though they may be explicitly only secular and natural.[9]

It might be added that Tillich's idea of the "theological circle" does not really bring him closer to Rahner's position. Although the situation lies within the theological circle and its questions receive direction and form from the message, it plays no positive role in providing answers because "the substance of the answers—the revelatory experience—is independent of the questions."[10] Such a dichotomy is foreign to Rahner. Therefore his mystagogy, based instead on a fundamental unity of experience and doctrine, is not an attempt to unite two independent realities. For this reason it is less likely to appear as indoctrination. It rather seeks to disclose the clues or intimations of divine grace already found in experience and to relate them to the meanings contained in the Christian tradition. Perhaps Rahner had Tillich's position in mind when he wrote: "God is already and always, in the offer of his self-communication in the Holy Spirit, in man as *the* question and *the* answer (in one), even when they remain unspoken, and . . . therefore the proclamation of the Gospel tells man only what he already *is*. . . ."[11]

In proclaiming the Christian message to people who do not spontaneously and naturally connect it with the mysterious depths of their own experience, the apologist can fruitfully apply the principles of a categorical mystagogy which organically relates experience and doctrine, which searches out the precise points of contact between the two, and which presents individual doctrines in relation to particular common human experiences.

II. TRANSCENDENTAL MYSTAGOGY

While a categorical mystagogy is important and will suffice in meeting the needs of some people, it does not respond to the radical nature of the contemporary problem of the eclipse of mystery. The fact is that many today are impervious to such an approach because they are so completely out of touch with a proper sense of mystery. It simply is not possible to match a doctrine with some perceived deeper experience because the experience itself has not entered explicit consciousness. In these cases a prior step is needed: the illumination and articulation of the religious dimension of human experience. This is in general the task of a transcendental mystagogy, and we should now examine it in greater detail.

1. We can gain an initial sense of the importance and meaning of this task by reflecting on how Christian apologists should proceed in dialogue with atheists who find the word 'God' meaningless and who think that human experience is exhausted by scientific data and logical deduction.[12]

Certain approaches are out of the question. The traditional Thomistic proofs for God's existence will not be effective because they conclude to the existence of a being which all are accustomed to designate by the word 'God', a point that secularized atheists will question. A simple effort to link experience and particular Christian doctrines is also going to fail because the atheistic interpretation of human experience will appear too truncated and superficial. For example, the Christian notion of resurrection cannot be presented in relation to people's deepest longings if they perceive the desires of their heart to be exhausted by the possibilities of this world. Even the more pragmatic argument that one cannot get along without God is of questionable value. The atheists may retort that there is no clear difference between the quality of life demonstrated by believers and nonbelievers, citing the virtuous lives and peaceful deaths of good people who never believed in God. They will simply assume that the constructive developments in our world have been achieved not by God but by people and that in the process religious beliefs have functioned mainly as a hindrance. If the apologists push the argument for the necessity of God, they are in danger of making God sound like a Freudian projection or a capriciously intervening being. The apologists must not speak of God in a way that sounds less respectful, less in touch with the negative side of life, less conscious of the limitations of language, than their atheistic dialogue partners.

Avoiding these ineffective approaches, the apologist must first become a mystagogue[13] by attempting to initiate atheists into a perception of the mystery dimension of their experience. It is a matter, not of transforming them into totally new persons, but of helping them come to a greater self-awareness, to an explicit consciousness of the religious dimension already present in their concrete lives. In attempting to disclose this experience the mystagogue must work within the atheists' horizon of self-understanding, use their vocabulary, and only employ presuppositions which are self-evident. The apologists are therefore working out of the premise that their dialogue partners have already had an experience of what is meant by God but for a variety of reasons cannot properly interpret their own experience or relate it to a theistic position.

In reflecting on the dialogue between Christian apologists and atheists who suffer from an eclipse of mystery we begin to see the outline of what transcendental mystagogy involves. The mystagogue, presupposing the graced condition of nonbelievers and respecting their intellectual framework, attempts to initiate them into a perception of the deeper dimensions of their experience.

2. We have spoken of the apologetic task of initiating into mystery. Let us now try to clarify the meaning of this "initiation" and the precise function of a transcendental mystagogy.

(a) The word 'initiation' can be misleading, since it may indicate an introduction into something totally new or alien. Actually the process is more accurately described by the term 'maieutic', taken in its common meaning of bringing latent ideas into explicit consciousness. Thus, mystogogy is, not an initiation into something external or the production of a new experience, but rather the disclosure of an experience that is already present, although in a hidden way. The maieutic process is one of awakening and activating a sense of the mystery which already rules our lives, of educating people toward a spontaneous realization of the significance of the ever-present deeper dimensions of life.

(b) We could think of the mystagogical task as a kind of spiritual depth psychology which understands that facing and accepting one's deeper experiences can be terribly frightening.[14] The difficulty of dealing with this anxiety indicates that mystagogues must be sensitive persons in touch with their own struggles and empathetic to the fears of those they address. The task is one of guiding and supporting others as they probe and express hidden and dark regions of themselves.

(c) This whole process should not be thought of as a type of indoctrination. Apologetics can fall into this trap by presenting doctrines as external truths unconnected with personal experience or as totally new ideas previously never considered by the persons addressed. Such an approach suggests the image of pouring something into an empty vessel. There is also a tendency in this method to subtle forms of manipulation based, for example, on arousing guilt feelings or invoking peer pressure. The term 'mystagogy', with both its unfamiliar character and its historical roots in sacramental initiation, could be helpful in overcoming the temptation to indoctrination. Mystagogues must avoid any semblance of pressure and any suggestion of a complete dichotomy between human experience and religious experience. They should realize that the truths they present may already have been accepted implicitly by their hearers and that no Christian doctrines are totally alien to common human experience. They must concentrate on inaugurating people into an experience of God that is always present, on awakening in them the sense of mystery which already pervades their existence, on gently inviting them to reflect on the genuine depths of their experience.

(d) Transcendental mystagogy involves overcoming a technical and utilitarian way of viewing the world while cultivating the ability to see the infinite in the finite. In a culture dominated by science there is a tendency to perceive reality in terms of objects to be measured and manipulated. Given this situation, the task of the mystagogue is to sharpen people's perception of the mystery that surrounds them, to encourage a type of meditative thinking that goes beyond rational calculation,[15] and to put people on alert for the echoes of the infinite in their ordinary experience.

(e) Initiating people into a sense of mystery requires that the deeper questions of life be raised to explicit consciousness. Mystagogues encounter the problem that many people today have repressed or inadequately articulated the ultimate questions of meaning, commitment, purpose, and the like. Therefore, Christian apologists cannot simply echo the more superficial questions of their contemporaries but must bring the great human questions to light and show that they are posed by existence itself and that people avoid them at their own peril.

(f) While mystagogy calls for a sharpened self-awareness, it must at the same time avoid the danger of excessive introspection. It is true that there is always more to be learned about our true motivations and the dark recesses of our unconscious. But there is also a destructive kind of unmasking of the self which views every achieved self-understanding as so incomplete as to be mere illusion. This can lead to a paralyzing examination of motivation and a cynical attitude toward the self which does indeed always exceed rational analysis. The danger of excessive introspection reminds us that a genuine mystagogy is not really an endless psychological self-analysis. It is interested in promoting self-awareness, but not in uncovering every hidden motivation. It encourages reflection on the ultimate questions but tries to avoid cynical self-doubt. It demands a certain trustful acceptance of the darkness of existence and a sense of the commonness of human nature in order to avoid such a solipsistic introspection. In short, transcendental mystagogy has the delicate task of encouraging self-reflection while avoiding an excessive preoccupation with self.

(g) It must be admitted that some people, for a variety of reasons, have an extremely diminished ability to trust the meaning of life and therefore are impervious to the ordinary methods of transcendental mystagogy.[16] Thus, for example, there are those who have undergone traumatic childhood experiences or have never achieved mutual loving relationships and therefore lack the experiential base for surrendering to the mystery of life and appreciating religious articulations. In these cases, mystagogy cannot consist of words alone. Fundamental trust must first be established through a loving relationship with another person who can serve as an effective model of confidence in the ultimate meaning of life. In other words, in extreme cases of psychic disturbance and emotional immaturity a transcendental mystagogy (whose main function is to disclose and articulate religious experience) will have to include a process of bringing to life or intensifying a trust that exists in an extremely tenuous and weakened condition. Even in this case it is a matter, not of indoctrination (on the model of filling an empty container), but of fostering an openness to the gracious mystery which is already present.

3. In all of these efforts to delineate the proper function of transcendental mystagogy a fundamental formal problem can be discerned: articulation does not match experience. The self-interpretation of individuals runs behind their self-experience. There are deeper levels of existence which are unrecognized, and important areas of human experience which remain unthematized.[17] In the face of this situation transcendental mystagogy tries to close the gap by awakening, disclosing, and articulating these deeper experiences. From another perspective it tries to correct, improve, and fill out faulty and incomplete self-interpretations.

In summary, the Christian apologist today often finds that even the most sophisticated categorical mystagogy is ineffective because the requisite deeper experiences of life are hidden. At this point the apologist must first become a mystagogue who attempts to bring to conscious awareness these experiences as a preliminary step before speaking of God and Christian doctrines. It is this transcendental mystagogy which will dominate our concern throughout the rest of the book.[18]

CHAPTER THREE

The Experience of Mystery

IF THE CHRISTIAN apologist is going to respond to the eclipse of mystery by disclosing "the deeper dimensions of life," it is essential to have a more precise understanding of those dimensions. In this chapter we will attempt to clarify exactly what it is that mystagogy is supposed to illumine and articulate. In other terms, we are trying to sharpen our understanding of what is commonly called "religious experience."

I. THE CATEGORY "SELF-EXPERIENCE"

It will prove helpful to conceive of this effort as an exploration of the full range and deepest dimensions of the experience of self. Self-experience, as used here, is in fact a central and all-embracing category. Rahner explains its inclusive character in this way:

> For when man, the subject, experiences himself as such, he is recognizing himself to be that particular being which is *quodammodo omnia*, not, that is to say, one particular subject among many others at the material level, but that inconceivable being in which the sum total of reality as such achieves realization of itself, so that the only way of fully understanding it would be to achieve an experience and understanding of reality itself.[1]

Self-experience is then wider than reflective self-knowledge, since we always experience more of ourselves than we are able to conceptualize or verbalize.

However, all experience remains self-experience because we do not undergo external events in a totally passive way, but we are personally modified by all of our encounters with reality. In this way absolutely nothing is, in principle, excluded from self-experience. A systematic study of this experience of self, such as should be done in metaphysical anthropology, is thus concerned with the totality of beings and with being in general. Therefore, the category "self-experience" appears as totally comprehensive, open to all reality, and capable of bearing within it distinctions, gradations, and nuances. In other words, we can begin to speak of structures and characteristics of this experience without worrying about excluding a priori some aspects of genuine religious experience.

It is important for our purposes to emphasize that "self-experience" is also a very dynamic category. It suggests, not a passive reception of an external piece of experience, but a self-enactment or a self-actuation.[2] We enact ourselves through our free acts, which means that we actively determine our very being and achieve an abiding validity for ourselves. We must take up a stand in relation to even the most determined elements in our existence; here again total passivity is ruled out. Thus, all experience has an active, dynamic character. Self-experience is self-actuation. It is difficult to convey this active sense in the term 'self-experience'. We could speak of the performance of experience, or the enactment of self-experience, or the act of self-experiencing. Whatever the language, the point is that our analysis is of active experiencing and not of static essences.

II. THE STRUCTURE OF SELF-EXPERIENCE

Self-experience is not a one-dimensional monolithic whole but possesses a nuanced structure. For example, we can discern within our experience of self various levels or degrees of existential involvement. Some acts seem to proceed from the very core of our being, to involve our whole person, to commit us totally, while others appear superficial, partial, and less demanding. Even the actions which flow from the center of the self only partially engage the various aspects or dimensions of one's personality. We may be committed to a project but find parts of our self rebelling against it, or we find that our fundamental decision for good is challenged by unintegrated aspects of our character. Our deepest personal responses achieve objectification only gradually throughout the various levels and aspects of our total personality. In short, we experience ourselves as more or less involved in, or committed to, particular actions, and we find that such inner experience has degrees of objectification or externalization.

A similar gradation can be discerned in terms of consciousness: we can have a vague, hazy awareness or a fully reflected and articulated awareness; our apprehension of reality can be simple and direct or mediated by reflexive concepts. Thus it is clear that our self-experience involves a differentiation of consciousness.

In trying to discern some structure in the various gradations of existential involvement and conscious awareness within self-experience I will employ Rahner's distinction between transcendental and categorical.[3] Since this distinction is central to his thought and crucial to understanding the mystagogical task, it bears full and careful explanation.

1. In general, Rahner employs the category "transcendental" in order to point to a dimension of human experience and a level of consciousness that is deeper, more important, and prior to the dimension of reflected, articulated, conceptualized experience which is termed 'categorical'.[4] Whenever he wants to refer to what stands behind the obvious world of clear propositions and external actions, he is inclined to use the word 'transcendental'. Often his intention is to remind his readers that real life is not limited to the clearly objectified realm and that all objectifications spring from a more primordial ground. Because he reacts against the tendency to idolize many diverse objectifications (dogma, sacraments, Church, propositional language, etc.), he uses the word 'transcendental' in a wide variety of contexts and with seemingly diverse meanings. In each case, however, his intention is to disclose the deeper realm behind the objectification.

In analyzing the relationship between the transcendental and categorical, it is possible to emphasize the distinction between these two levels of consciousness. Thus, it is one thing to have vague and unarticulated self-understanding, and quite another to be able to conceptualize precisely and articulate clearly who we are. In some ways the deepest levels of our self-experience seem beyond expression, and all our attempts at articulation appear quite inadequate. In fact, as we struggle to learn to understand and communicate our deepest experiences, we sense that there is an essential disparity between our immediate experience of self and every effort to articulate it. Each concrete expression of our perceived identity is necessarily placed within a larger horizon of self-understanding which always eludes precise definition. In short, we always know more about ourselves than we are able to say. For example, lovers know more about love in a direct and immediate way than any theory could explain or words capture.

In emphasizing that there are very distinct forms of human consciousness ranging from vague awareness to clear objectification, it is important to remember that we are not dealing with distinct regions which have to be somehow united. There is one human consciousness and a single unified experience of self which only subsequently can be distinguished into levels or dimensions. The transcendental and the categorical are necessarily and essentially related, and healthy self-experience involves a continuing interaction between them. Reflexive consciousness without its transcendental grounding withers; transcendental awareness without its objectification is blind. A proper image of this relationship is, not two spheres placed side by side, but one circle of human experience with two poles dialectically related. In working out this dialectical relationship a certain primacy is to be given to the transcendental. Categorical experience is always the historical self-interpretation of the transcendental experience, which is itself the actuation of the being of a person. Reflection and objectification are necessary but remain secondary to what a person actually experiences in life. To return to the example of the immediate awareness of lovers, it is also true that their love always involves some type of reflexive self-knowledge and that the various expressions of this love have a power to enliven and enrich it.

2. To continue our exposition of the structure of self-experience, let us discuss the transcendental realm itself more fully. There are certain inescapable fundamental human experiences which are distinguished from our sensible experience of objects and which are in some way known prior to any reflection on them. For example, we experience what joy, pain, love, anxiety, and trust are before we ever reflect on them in an explicit way. Such experiences can deepen and grow or be denied and atrophy. They can be more or less adequately reflected and expressed. However, they remain, in some way, part of our self-awareness. This is true even though they are known, not as objects or by introspection, but only in their actual performance. They involve a type of knowledge which is closely bound up with the very foundations of our existence. A good indication of the existence of this mode of knowing is found in the fact that persons who argue logically already know in some way what logic is even if they cannot articulate the rules of logic.

I think one problem in understanding Rahner's discussion of transcendental experience is that he allows the term to slide between two referents: a certain fundamental experience of life and the co-consciousness that such experience involves. In the first instance he is directing our attention to the primacy of what we could call "lived experience." He is stressing the simple (if often forgotten) truth that how we respond to life is more important than how we describe it, that experiencing comes before verbalization, and that lived experience is always richer than any of its objectifications. Second, he is claiming that we have a type of awareness of this lived experience which is more fundamental than our conceptual knowledge. The mere existence of such a transcendental awareness should be acceptable to people today who have learned from depth psychology that verbalized awareness does not exhaust the psychic life. In fact, it seems self-evident that there is a difference between our free, unthematic self-possession and our conceptualized self-interpretation. However, the problem comes when we try to describe and explain this deeper awareness since it cannot be detached from concrete categorical experience and is not encountered as a particular object. We could speak of co-consciousness since our self-experience is so structured that in all of our knowing and willing, particular objects are enfolded in a larger awareness. We could perhaps call it a state of consciousness which has not yet been made explicit. It is like a mood or a vague feeling. It has been variously described as an inner luminosity in which we know particular objects, an atmosphere or space in which we encounter particular things, a basic disposition which accompanies all our knowing.[5] This transcendental awareness is the kind of knowledge which lies on the edge of our consciousness and which, if it breaks into explicit awareness, produces the reaction that we seem to have known it all along. It is a knowledge that accompanies our very existence as human beings and colors our perception of reality. It is the light which makes the knowledge of all objects possible, but itself is not known as an object.

Our discussion of transcendental experience provides us with vital insights and a helpful terminology in understanding religious experience. Lived experience is prior to all reflection and remains richer than every effort to capture it in words. At the same time self-experience truly does include a co-consciousness which can legitimately be described in cognitive terms as a type of preconceptual awareness. Since this co-knowledge is not of a particular object but is the condition for all knowing, it can be described as a mood or disposition. To avoid the implication that is it a distinct realm of consciousness, we could speak of it as a dimension of our unified self-awareness. Finally, to stress its primacy and hidden character, it can be termed the depth dimension of our human experience.

3. Our great emphasis on transcendental awareness could suggest that we are neglecting or undervaluing the concrete historical aspects of existence. As a proper counterpoint we should note that lived experience seeks objectification. We realize or achieve ourselves, not in an abstract spiritualized inwardness, but in external

interaction with other persons and with our environment. Transcendental awareness has the tendency to manifest itself in all the dimensions of human self-experience. Rahner stated the point strongly:

> There are in fact *no purely internal* processes in a properly metaphysical sense. . . . Everything, even the innermost human matters, are still corporeal, dependent on the material and thus on something already directed towards the external world, something objectified . . .; everything in our innermost being is directed towards the outside and finds its resonance in the world of things. . . . Hence, man objectifies himself and his inner outlook, his original free decision and attitude '*ad extra*'; . . . The external activity is not always merely a subsequent announcement and a secondary consequence of this internal decision, but just as frequently (indeed in the last analysis, always, to some extent) it is that in which alone the internal act can be achieved and posited.[6]

In other words, self-experience is always and necessarily bodily, social, and historical. A purely spiritual, individual, unhistorical self-actuation is impossible. Although the various objectifications in concept, language, symbol, action, and such can never exhaust this transcendental dimension, they do reflect it and can modify and intensify it. The very attempt to objectify experience already modifies the experience itself, setting up a continuing history of the development of the self through the interaction of the transcendental and the categorical. We find a model for this interaction in the life shared by two lovers. Their love sustains and colors all their interactions, and yet at times this love must be expressed in word and gesture which in turn enriches the original love. Love achieves itself through gestures which are themselves not the love but are necessary lest love die. The experience of love then has a history which results from the interaction of lived experience and its objectification.

Let us try to deepen our understanding of the essential and necessary role of the categorical in self-experience by examining two of Rahner's important ideas on persons and their knowing. The first is that all conceptualization includes an imaginative element.[7] Even the most metaphysical or spiritual knowledge involves the work of imagination. The point is that human consciousness necessarily possesses a transcendental-categorical structure because we are finite spirit, and our knowing must include both the light of the intellect and a concrete image. A sort of pure transcendental knowing is impossible precisely because there is no thought without image. Our categorical experience is structured by these images and by their com-

bination into picturesque language and into myths. Our conceptualization is tied to particular imaginative representations. As thought
develops, it can find expression in alternate images, but it can never
be replaced by an imageless language. Human growth is facilitated by
a progressively better formulation of who we are and by new images
and symbols which help to structure our experience in a coherent
way. Hence, reflection and its various imaginative formulations are
not outside of or in addition to experience but are necessary compo-
nents of experience itself.

The second consideration which helps ground the categorical
dimension is Rahner's notion that humans are symbolic beings.[8] This
assertion means not only that we use symbols to express and structure our world but that we are symbolic creatures in our very constitution. This arises from the fact that the body is the symbol of the
soul inasmuch as it is the self-realization of the soul. The soul makes
itself present and visible in the body, which itself is the actuality of
the soul but remains distinct from it. We not only have a body but
are our bodies. This is a very dynamic notion in which we are not
simply collapsed into a static homogeneous identity but possess a
mixture of richness and limitation which requires us to express and
achieve ourselves successively in acts of knowledge and love. In
every human expression the whole person is present, actuating the
self in and through bodiliness. These bodily objectifications are not
arbitrary but represent the only way that we can actuate our basic
orientation and thus ultimately achieve our self.

Seeing human existence as symbolic gives us a dynamic picture
of persons gradually realizing themselves in a plurality of external
objectifications, while at the same time maintaining their essential
unity as a bodied spirit.

If we are essentially imaginative knowers and symbolic creatures, then there is a solid foundation for claiming that the categorical
dimension is a necessary part of a differentiated human consciousness. Then self-experience cannot be restricted to the transcendental
realm in a false otherworldly escapism but must be seen as necessarily
concrete, imaginative, bodily, social, and historical.

Our rather lengthy discussion of the relationship between transcendental and categorical enables us to gain a better grasp of the
structure of self-experience as a single differentiated consciousness
within which the two dimensions are dialectically related. There is a
genuine transcendental awareness which always and necessarily ob-
jectifies itself in various degrees ranging from vague mood through
initial reflection, verbalization, symbolic expression, and external ac-

tion. From this perspective the mystagogical task can be seen as disclosing the depths of transcendental experience and facilitating a gradually clearer and more complete categorical objectification. In other words, the mystagogue must help people get in touch with their deeper, more primordial lived experience and articulate and symbolize it more accurately.

III. SELF-EXPERIENCE AND MYSTERY

1. If mystagogy is going to be something more than the elaboration of a self-enclosed humanism, then we have to find within self-experience an essential orientation to the transcendent. In theological terms we must establish and elucidate the thesis that the experience of self necessarily involves the experience of God.[9] The fundamental insight of this proposition can be expressed in various ways.

Persons as spiritual subjects possess an essential reference to absolute mystery which is always present whether they explicitly recognize it or not and whether they accept it or reject it. In other words, in our knowing and free action we unavoidably point beyond individual objects to an infinite horizon which cannot be comprehended within our usual frame of reference. In this formulation the notion of self-experience becomes a little more specific, since it is said to consist of acts of knowledge and freedom; while the reference point is less specific, since it is described as absolute mystery rather than being designated by the more concrete term 'God'.

We could also express our thesis in terms of the experience of transcendence and its source. This suggests that our self-experience always includes an intentional surpassing of individual limitations and raises the question about the source of this power. Again, this is a very open-ended way of formulating the thesis and allows for further specification of the two terms.

Finally, and most helpfully, we can speak of our transcendentality and its term or goal. We are creatures of infinite openness in all dimensions of our lives and possess a dynamism that exceeds every conceivable limit in a movement toward an infinite goal. The term 'transcendentality' is helpful because it invites a consideration of all the ways that our spiritual nature might actuate itself. By describing the reference point as the goal the question as to its precise nature is kept open.

2. Let us now try to clarify our understanding of human tran-

scendentality. We find in ourselves an unlimited receptivity, an openness to the whole of reality, an ability to receive which is not exhausted by any particular object. This more passive potentiality is complemented by a dynamic striving in which our knowing and willing are never brought to rest by any particular achievement but constantly press toward the infinite. Thus we can characterize our transcendentality as "spirit" to indicate both a receptive potentiality for all being and a dynamic desire for the whole of reality.

This general analysis suggests that we will experience our transcendentality in a twofold manner. First, there is the encounter with limitation. Finite objects cannot fill our infinite horizon, no amount of knowledge is ever enough, and personal relationships never totally satisfy. These experiences of limit[10] are concretized and sharpened by the tragic experiences of life such as failed love, suffering, sickness, and the final limit: death. In these boundary situations[11] we experience ourselves as limited, finite, and contingent. However, we can only experience these events as limit because in some way we have already transcended them. Thus one dimension of our transcendentality is revealed to us as we run up against our ordinary limitations and the boundary situations in life. These experiences can also raise the question of the source of the dynamism which finds limits frustrating.

The second modality of human transcendence is more positive and points to our experience of overflowing any particular object in a drive toward the infinite. In this case the stress is on the surpassing rather than the limit. It brings to mind more the joy of striving and the excitement of encountering the new. It is a matter of more intensive experiences which press upon our consciousness the question of transcendence. In some respects we can speak of these as "peak-experiences"[12] in which we know the peace and integrity of moving into closer union with the goal of our striving. In these cases we experience ourselves as surpassing the ordinary finite world in a dynamic reaching out toward a goal which is perceived as gracious. Without further pursuing the question of the nature of the goal we have at least indicated that we experience our transcendentality not only as a negative "ontological shock"[13] resulting from the encounter of limits and contingency but also as an ecstatic experience[14] in which we intentionally surpass all limits.

How are we to understand the relationship between our transcendentality and its goal? It seems important to establish first of all a primordial unity between the subjective and objective poles of our experience. In other words, our spiritual dynamism and its infinite goal can only be properly understood as dialectically related in an essential unity. This is not simply an exemplification of the principle that knowing involves an identification of knower and known. Its deepest significance lies rather in the fact that the experience of the goal is the enabling condition without which no experience of self is even possible. The point could also be formulated from the other side. The experience of self is the enabling condition of the experience of the goal since we can only have a transcendental awareness of the goal of our striving to the degree that we have achieved our own subjectivity. In either formulation it is important to remember that the experience of the infinite goal is not one experience among others but is the unifying factor and the very essence of all our personal experience. Without a transcendental experience of the goal of our dynamic spirit we could not even be aware of ourselves as a spiritual subject. Transcendentality can only be understood in terms of its goal. Self-awareness necessarily involves an implicit awareness of mystery.

While stressing this primordial unity, we must be on guard against an easy identification of self-experience and the experience of God or of an absolute identity which would lead to pantheism. The experience of our transcendentality as a gift seems to preclude an identification with the absolute mystery. The fact that our questioning is unlimited and our desire for love is never satisfied clearly indicates we are creatures and not God. Once we have established this distance, we can safely return to our thesis that self-experience is the experience of God with its clear intent to convey an ultimate, primordial, and all-embracing unity between our spiritual dynamism and its infinite goal. Thus our transcendentality always includes and is encompassed by an experience of mystery even when it is repressed, forgotten, or denied. By examining human transcendence we arrive at a better understanding of our self-experience. It appears as infinite openness to a source which supports us and drives us past all limits, and as a dynamic striving for a goal which draws and encompasses us. Self-experience is the experience of God.

3. Having seen the general structure of our transcendentality, we can now examine its concrete manifestations. Where do we look? First of all, to our self-experience. But what kind of experience? The first answer is: any and all of our encounters with reality. God is equally near and can be found in every conceivable existential situation. Our transcendentality can be mediated or actuated by any categorical reality which acts as a catalyst for our self-realization. There are no exclusive spheres of religious experience; on the contrary, the

whole world is potentially revelatory. In our concrete existence we continuously encounter the infinite goal often without being explicitly aware of it. Rahner is helpful here because he provides numerous descriptions of religious experience with the avowed purpose of evoking a responsive chord in his readers and bringing to conceptual awareness the mystery which lies hidden.[15] For example, he speaks of the experience of grace in terms of "indescribable joy, unconditional personal love, unconditional obedience to conscience, the experience of loving union with the universe, the experience of the irretrievable vulnerability of one's own human existence beyond one's own control."[16]

In comparing these descriptions or mystagogical passages[17] we find certain types of experience reappearing: facing death, bearing the responsibility of freedom, sensing radical joy and hope, experiencing great love, undergoing unquenchable discontent and anxiety, being faithful to conscience, and giving selflessly without receiving. Although any experience can mediate transcendence, it is clear that some experiences have a greater potential to do so. This suggests the need to discern the "privileged experiences" which have a special power to mediate mystery to people today.

Among these, special prominence can be given to situations in which we are thrown back upon ourselves and can no longer evade the deeper questions of life. These occurrences have a striking, paradoxical, and shattering character even though they may appear very ordinary.[18] Our usual modes of socially programmed perception are shaken, and ordinary thinking cannot adequately comprehend the situation.[19] This can happen in very simple ways. For example, a person makes a sacrifice without any reasonable hope for earthly reward, or faces extreme loneliness, or senses the heavy burden of freedom, or comes face to face with death.[20] In all such experiences a person's existence is revealed as contingent, as incomprehensible in ordinary terms, and as open to the transcendent.

Interpersonal relationships of love form a second type of privileged experience. The deepest reason for this is that personal relationships are the necessary and essential condition of any achievement of self-realization. Although knowledge of things has an importance, a genuine experience of self is possible only in and through personal encounter. In addition, when these relationships involve mutual love, they have a surprising ability to reveal a sense of mystery. For example, a man experiences a mysterious exhilaration when he realizes that he is accepted in an unconditional love that far exceeds what he deserves. Human love clearly possesses a special power to open up the deeper dimensions of self-experience.

4. The emphasis we have been putting on the transcendental dimension raises again the question about the necessity and value of categorical religious experience. How can any religious objectifications have real significance if in our transcendental self-experience we are already directly related to God? The difficulty is exacerbated by the fact that many people today feel that a respectful silence is the proper response to the mystery that pervades their existence. There is a reticence to speak about the deepest matters, a fear of one's religious language being misunderstood, and a delicate sense of the inadequacy of all symbolization of the religious dimension. With this whole problem in mind we should now discuss the more objective and explicit aspects of religious experience.

As we have seen, there is never a pure transcendental experience, and so we can assume that religious experience must always have at least an incipient categorical element which is open to a gradually more complete objectification. Thus, we could imagine a person beginning with an experience of infinite longings, interpreting it as coming from a gracious source, naming this source God, accepting the doctrine that God has come near in the person of Jesus of Nazareth, joining the visible community that professes this belief, celebrating this presence in the Eucharist, and finally living out this belief in a life of charity. We have here an example of a progressively greater objectification in Christian terms of a transcendental experience. The actualizing of each of these stages could be termed "categorical religious experience," and it is important to establish its value and function.

(a) Religious objectifications have the power to enrich transcendental experience. Without them we could never be certain about the precise nature of the mystery which supports us and our world.[21] The very ambiguity of our experience could lead to excessively negative interpretations. Lacking adequate verbalization, even our positive insights can get fuzzy and doubt can take over. In addition, the categorical can have a formative influence by deepening, intensifying, and broadening the experience of transcendence. For example, when our fundamental trust is shaken or threatened, the biblical account of the faithfulness of Jesus or the fellowship of a eucharistic celebration can strengthen and heal this basic disposition.[22] Finally, the various objectifications have the power to free us from hidden self-destructive tendencies and to initiate us into a new liberating self-awareness by revealing to us the deepest sources of our personal existence.

(b) The necessity and value of categorical religious experience can also be argued on the theological grounds that grace seeks visibility.[23] Since God's self-giving, which we call grace, reaches its high point in the historical incarnation of the Word, it follows that all grace has a propensity toward a perceptible manifestation. This indicates that grace, which is everywhere present in our world, is meant to touch all dimensions of human life including the visible and social. It should not stay locked up in the hidden core of a person, but should flow into external activity and a common life shared with others. Thus the categorical expression of grace is not an arbitrary peripheral matter but is of the very essence of a full religious experience.

(c) The various religious objectifications can be a positive aid to salvation. Rahner argues that the acceptance of the totality of Christian doctrine has the greatest potential for facilitating the achievement of a transcendental relationship to God.

> Yet one will nevertheless be able to say that, if the unfolded fullness of articulated truths of faith is to have any significance at all for a successful inner attitude of faith—a possibility which cannot reasonably be denied (although faith, grace, justification and thus the whole reality of faith referred to, may already be present even when there is merely belief in the existence of God: Heb. 11:6)—then it cannot be denied that basically and *ceteris paribus* one must give a greater chance of real existential belief and thus of attaining the whole reality of salvation (in grace) to someone who adheres more explicitly, more clearly and in a more articulate way to the greater part of the Christian propositions of faith and who still aims explicitly at the Christian reality which he has encountered historically and which he calls 'by name' (whereby he has a real relationship to it which is still—in part—independent of the fact as to how he interprets this reality).[24]

This positive appraisal of the value of a fully articulated Christian faith has to be carefully understood. It reminds us of the power of explicit Christianity to stir up the depths of faith, to strengthen flagging commitments, and to articulate clearly genuine religious sentiments which are only vaguely understood. However, this must be placed in the larger context of the possibility of salvation for all those who are faithful to their conscience, and be balanced by the fact that the gift of a reflective religious awareness does not seem to be given to everyone.[25] Within this framework it does seem that the optimum situation is a fruitful interaction between a positive lived relationship with God and various religious objectifications which illumine, strengthen, and celebrate this existential reality.

In summary, the necessity and value of the categorical dimension of religious experience are suggested by the nature of the inter-action between the transcendental and categorical, by the tendency of grace to seek visibility, and finally by its function as an aid to salvation. Taken together these three justifications could constitute the outline of a response to the silent believers and the admonition of Wittgenstein to remain silent about such mysterious matters which defy clear language.[26] Thus, we could say that while Wittgenstein's dictum has indeed captured an authentic aspect of contemporary understanding—that is, the reticence to speak about mystery—it fails to do justice to a human transcendentality which seeks expression and in turn is nourished by religious objectifications.

This line of thought also serves as a justification for the mystagogical effort to help people move from a transcendental to a categorical awareness. Human beings are impoverished by a lack of proper religious objectifications since they are then prey to unrecognized demons and unaware of the deepest sources of their joys in life.[27] The fact that we are already in touch with the mystery should not prevent us from looking for the explicit interpretation which expresses clearly what we have vaguely sensed and often misunderstood.

5. Having discussed the subjective pole of religious experience, we now turn our attention to the objective pole. We want to concentrate on the reference point and enabling condition of the human experience of transcendence. It is a matter of trying to discern the nature of the source and goal of our spiritual dynamism. Classical theology discussed this question under the heading of the attributes of God. However, it seems better to frame the question, at least initially, in more neutral terms by asking about the nature and characteristics of the mysterious goal of our strivings. One reason for adopting this approach is that the word 'God' is itself problematic. For some it is a meaningless word, while for others it already says too much since it prejudges the question of the nature of the goal of our strivings in favor of graciousness, personal character, and so on. Another reason for beginning with neutral language is that it guarantees a thoroughly anthropocentric approach by sending us back to human experience as the starting point. To inquire about a goal turns us immediately to the experience of striving towards it. When we ask about the attributes of God, it seems easier to neglect experience and to think of God as a separate object or being whose characteristics can be objectively investigated.

Let us now try to fill out our understanding of the term or goal of human transcendence.[28]

(a) The goal is not an object or a particular being that falls within our ordinary system of coordinates. Our experience is that we strive beyond all finite objects toward a hidden term which we never comprehend or directly perceive. We know this goal only as the condition which makes our spiritual activity possible. It is never directly perceived but is co-known as the fundamental basis for all our knowing and willing.

Therefore, the goal of our transcendence in one sense must remain "nameless." Names limit, divide, and assign specific characteristics, while the goal cannot be described in terms of anything else nor fit into a larger frame of reference in which it could be assigned a particular place. It functions as the condition of the possibility for the naming of all individual objects and, as such, cannot itself be named. In calling it "nameless" we are able to highlight its distinction from all objects that have names. The goal can be described as "indefinable" or "unlimitable" because it functions as an infinite horizon within which particular realities can be known and loved. Since it is the condition for all spiritual activity, it cannot be contained in some other larger horizon. It is the space within which all realities are distinguished and, as such, is not subject to this distinguishing. Therefore, we can say that the term is not only unlimited but in principle is unlimitable. The boundary which limits all things cannot itself be enclosed within some more comprehensive boundary.

Finally, we must remember that the goal of transcendence is beyond all our capability to control, manipulate, or comprehend. It is present as a gift that exceeds our powers to pin it down or to capture it in a net of concepts. In short, it is not at our disposal but disposes of us.

In summary, the term of our transcendentality is clearly not an object that can be named, defined, or controlled. It is rather the point of reference for all naming, the enabling condition for all defining, and the infinite source of all disposing.

(b) The goal can be fruitfully discussed in terms of "mystery."[29] This term has the advantage of sounding nonobjective and of inviting further investigation into its real nature and character. It can also have a more evocative and involving tone to it than the dry, abstract philosophical language of "being" or "ground of being."[30]

Of course, it is important to understand the word 'mystery' properly if it is going to function effectively. It should not be thought of as the object of a rational investigation which will eventually comprehend it. An authentic notion of mystery must be derived from our experience of responding to life from a point deeper than our rational faculties. If we think of the way we know our beloved ones, we realize that reason is subsumed into a more primordial kind of knowing. We are responding out of a center or deeper unified point that undercuts the usual distinction between reason and will. Our knowledge then moves beyond logical deduction and achieves a greater depth when it is transformed by a love which surrenders to the uniqueness of the other. It is in this experience that a dimension of mystery appears which transcends all rational calculation. We come to know what genuine mystery is by reflecting on just this type of experience rather than by contemplating a particularly elusive object.

From this analysis it is clear that the word 'mystery' should first be applied to the goal of transcendence which is essentially unknowable, and not to a temporary unknown which is waiting for reason to overtake and comprehend it. The goal of our transcendentality is well described as mystery since it permanently remains beyond our comprehension and control. It is precisely in our single unified experience of transcendentality with its infinite horizon that we come to know what the word 'mystery' means. It is a question, not of bringing in some concept from outside this experience and applying it to an object which is denominated as "mystery," but of finding within human experience a dynamic tendency toward an infinite horizon which is properly designated "mystery." In short, the experience of self-transcendence is the paradigm for understanding mystery.

(c) The mysterious term of human transcendence can be named the "gracious mystery." When we reflect on our spiritual dynamism as the power of freedom and love, we move into the more personal area of values and commitment. We experience our freedom primarily in personal relationships in which the love offered by the other person is a condition of possibility for our own self-realization. When this analysis is applied to our experience of a transcending love involving an infinite mystery, it seems proper to describe the mystery in terms of a loving partner. It is perceived as the benign source and enabling condition of our own capability of achieving genuine love. When the goal is conceived according to a personalistic model as the source of love, it seems fitting to characterize it as "gracious." Again we should note that this designation is derived from the experience of a friendly transcending goal and is not imported from outside this experience and subsequently attributed to the mystery. "Gracious mystery," therefore, remains a transcendental designation and is not a strict definition of the infinite goal since there is nothing outside of it in terms of which it could be defined. It really functions as an indication that the mystery which always surrounds us is personal and trustworthy.

(d) The mystery does not remain distant but draws near to us. We experience our infinite longings, not as an autonomous self-contained power of our own, but as a drive initiated by a goal that remains beyond our control. Our clear hope is that this goal does not remain totally inaccessible but that a union which brings ultimate fulfillment is possible. Some people seem to interpret this hope as an absurd longing for a goal which is best described as a void or nothingness. Our thesis that the mystery draws near is a more positive interpretation, which suggests that the goal not only is trustworthy but wants to initiate and accomplish a personal union with us. When this notion receives its full Christian expression, we have the doctrine of Incarnation. This notion that God has manifested himself in Jesus of Nazareth suggests a positive interpretation of our often ambiguous experience: that the mysterious goal of our longings is not a distant horizon but a personal and loving nearness.

IV. CHARACTERISTICS OF RELIGIOUS EXPERIENCE

We have been trying to clarify our understanding of the religious dimension of self-experience. It will be helpful at this point to gather some of its characteristics in schematic form.

1. The self-experience of every person inescapably contains a religious dimension whether it is conscious or not, accepted or rejected, rightly or wrongly interpreted. Hence it is available to everyone and not just a privileged few, or the explicitly religious. It is more fundamental than all rational calculation about it since it is the necessary condition of all knowing. Talk of a religious dimension points to the radicalizing of our transcendentality since it suggests the presence of an empowering goal which directs our dynamism toward itself.

2. Religious experience has a paradoxical character. It is not a matter of a sentimental joy or cheap grace. There is no pure experience of transcendence apart from a concomitant experience of limitation. The positive side of the experience presupposes the negative and must be seen as a triumph over it. Appreciating religious experience necessarily involves learning to see light in the midst of darkness, to hear a positive word out of the silence, to feel loved when depressed, to find life in death.

3. It is possible to speak of degrees of religious experience even though it is an inescapable experience of all people. There is a common structure found in religious experience, but it can involve gradations ranging from ordinary experiences of grace to mystical states. The differentiation is explained by the various degrees of free acceptance of the ever-present source of human transcendence. Even when it is totally rejected, it continues to affect transcendental experience. In addition, the affirmative appropriation of it can be increased, deepened, and intensified. Thus, there are degrees of existential closeness to the mystery.

The other source of gradation in religious experience is the ability to reflect on it and to objectify it. Some people are more in touch with their deepest experience and have a greater ability to verbalize it: the poet and the mystic, for example. Others are in close existential contact with the mystery of life but have very little ability to either reflect on it or verbalize it. Therefore, we can posit various degrees of both existential and reflected religious experience.

4. Although there are unchanging elements in religious experience, it is also true that a particular historical and cultural situation stamps the experience as well as the form of its objectification. In other words, the culture affects the initial experience itself as well as the language that people use to describe it. Today the culture seems to produce many people who tend to experience the transcendent as the goal and source of human activity rather than as a divine being who intervenes periodically in human history. For them the principal mediating factor of religious experience is not the external world but their experience of the mystery of their own existence. Thus, struggling with the burden of freedom, trying to establish authentic personal relationships, and working toward self-acceptance seem to have a special power to reveal personal limitations and to evoke a sense of mystery.

5. It is possible to discern two general types or modes of religious experience: the encounter with limitation and the union with gracious mystery. In the first we are very conscious of our limitations, our essential contingency, our dependency on a power greater than ourselves. We sense the huge gap between our longings and our finite capabilities. There is an initial negative flavor to this experience since we have to face the painful reality that we do not control our own existence and must find our fulfillment outside of ourselves. However, in being thrown back on our finite selves we are also given the opportunity of experiencing the liberating power of submitting to the mystery that lovingly supports and draws us.

In the second type we are more conscious of our union with the gracious mystery. We know the peace and integration that comes from living in harmony with this mystery. We are conscious that our strivings are bringing us closer to a gracious goal and that the process of life can be trusted because it has a benign source. In its most complete manifestation this is the ecstatic experience of intense union known as mysticism. But even in its less spectacular forms it retains its joyful and positive character. Of course, these two types should not sharply be distinguished since they are really modes (one of which predominates) of a unified religious experience which is always a mixture of both.

6. Religious experience necessarily involves a dynamic interplay of the transcendental and categorical realms. A pure, unmediated angelic experience is impossible for us human beings. Transcendental experience is always embedded in the imaginative, bodily, social dimension of human existence. At the same time there is no authentic, objective, external religious experience apart from the involvement of the deeper dimensions of the individual. The categorical must flow from the genuine sentiments of the heart and in turn has the power to nourish this transcendental dimension.

7. Religious experience necessarily includes the subjective pole of human transcendence and the objective pole of the gracious mystery. We cannot properly understand our infinite longings apart from the goal toward which they tend. We come to know the nature and characteristics of the personal mystery which grounds our existence by reflecting on our spiritual dynamism. Our unified human experience is essentially relational, and its true religious depths only appear as we become more aware of our subjectivity and gradually fill out our understanding of its mysterious source and goal.

CHAPTER FOUR

Disclosing Mystery

HOW IS THE MYSTAGOGUE to carry out the task of disclosing and articulating the religious dimension of self-experience for those who are impoverished by the eclipse of mystery? Here we will present a series of methodological suggestions which can guide this enterprise.

1. Mystagogy should make use of the valid insights of the secular culture. It should be prepared to tap the sources of religious experience found in the modern world and to enter into dialogue with the various self-understandings available today. This effort could be described as a search for the meanings common both to modern secular consciousness and to a theistic self-interpretation.[1] We could also think of it as a thematization in religious terms of the authentic values of modernity.[2] For example, mystagogy could find a fruitful dialogue partner in the so-called "third force in psychology"[3] or in humanistic sociology.[4] Mystagogues, in drawing on the human sciences, should be prepared to resist the tendency of science to make comprehensive claims and to evolve into a total world view. In fact, there can be no ultimate conflict between science which deals with particular areas of human experience and a theism which speaks of the totality of existence and the ground of all experience. Therefore, the insights of the sciences can be appropriated into a religious outlook and their validity judged within a larger meaning system.

Not only can valuable insights be gained from the sciences, but science itself can have a mystagogical function. This occurs when the scientific enterprise leads to a recognition of its own limitations and to a sense of awe or wonder in the face of a vast, complex, and ultimately mysterious universe. It also happens when scientists are moved to ask deeper and more comprehensive questions: for example, whether a harmonious universe has an intelligent source, whether there is a comprehensive horizon within which science fits, and whether there is a transcending purpose in scientific work.

When these questions are taken seriously, then the scientific enterprise itself reveals a dimension of mystery that calls for some type of religious articulation—indeed mystagogy in action.

Science, because of its great influence on contemporary self-consciousness, is a particularly important dialogue partner for the mystagogue, but it is not the only one. Actually, the apologist must break out of a closed religious ghetto and search all aspects of modern culture for intimations of mystery.[5] This is no easy task, as Michael Novak, commenting on the American scene, reminds us:

> The task of ferreting out empirical, experiential evidences of transcendence in American life requires something akin to genius. For to accomplish it well is to combine the poet's and novelist's and politician's sense of fact, detail and incident with sustained reflection and analytic precision. Moreover, one must have a fox's eye for irony and self-deception.[6]

Nonetheless, mystagogy must make the effort to uncover and utilize the genuine values and insights of the contemporary culture.

2. Mystagogy should make use of evocative language in order to disclose mystery effectively. It is a matter, not of indoctrination based on the model of filling an empty container, but of trying to describe the experience of mystery in the hope that the listeners will then discover it in themselves. The proper tone or mood is one of invitation, in which persons are asked to judge whether the description finds an echo in their own experience. In other words, the sense of mystery "cannot, strictly speaking, be taught, it can only be evoked, awakened in the mind."[7]

In searching for the proper language to do this, two problems can be discerned: if the descriptions are very concrete and personalized, then there is a danger that they are judged too poetic and individualistic; if the language is philosophically exact, it sounds too abstract and can be judged as a mere playing with words and concepts. In response to the first problem, we should note that there is empirical evidence to show that vivid, colorful descriptions of deep experiences have the capacity to evoke a positive response of recognition in other people.[8] This can occur because all language is rooted in concrete human living and personal interaction.[9]

Words are not mere external sounds nor arbitrary signals but rather the embodiment of thought and the mode of personal presence. Some words, it is true, explain reality by breaking it up into segments, and their function is to give us mastery over things. Since they are clear and nonmysterious, they can be called "technical words." However, other words tend to unite, to conjure up the whole, to have power over us, to open up the finite to the infinite, and to lead to reverence before the mystery. Such words can be termed "primordial."[10] A good example of a primordial word is 'heart',[11] which originates in the experience of people and cannot be defined in terms of other better-known words. It refers in a concrete way to the essential unity of individuals before any split into body and soul or reason and emotion. The heart represents the center point where an individual encounters God. Such primordial words, while pointing to a concrete reality, also have a strange power to evoke mystery, to open up a transcendent realm, to suggest the presence of the infinite in the finite. In other words, they have both a literal and a transcending meaning. They reflect the organic unity of all reality and make that reality present to the hearer. When touched by these words, individuals experience themselves as grasped by the reality signified.

This insight into the evocative power of primordial words can be formulated in other ways. We could speak of the power of theological language to awaken a person to the encounter with holy Being and to illumine existence at its deepest levels.[12] It could be expressed as the power of the limit-language of the Christian gospel to disclose the mysterious possibilities of authentic human existence.[13] The insight can also be expressed in terms of the power of Christian symbols to give shape and tone to the horizon of ultimacy which always encompasses man.[14] Even among those influenced by the analytic tradition we find a similar idea: namely, that religious language has the ability to disclose situations of "odd discernment" and "total commitment."[15]

In each of these formulations there is a recognition of the power of nonliteral expressions to open up a transcendent realm. They suggest that a transcendental mystagogy must take the risk of employing a vivid, symbolic, poetic language even though it may be open to the charge of meaninglessness and unverifiability.

As regards the other problem of conceptual language appearing too dry and abstract, we should note that proper conceptualization can also evoke and thematize mystery. For example, a carefully formulated creed can move people to prayerful reflection and summon them to search out the experiential basis in their own lives for the various statements of the creed. Even traditional dogmas—with all their cultural conditioning, defensive purpose, and often alien categories—can be presented as pointing to the infinite mystery which remains beyond all words. While it must be admitted that many people find precise philosophical language to be either unintelligible or dull, there are some who are moved to deeper personal reflection by precisely formulated and tightly argued analyses of human experience.

In this discussion it is interesting to note the evocative character of the word 'God'.[16] The very existence of this word is fascinating, and we might ponder what would happen if it disappeared. Then people would no longer be confronted with the whole of their existence. They would forget themselves completely and be totally immersed in the superficial details of their lives. They would no longer be able to transcend themselves and would cease to be genuinely human, having returned to the animal state. This suggests the positive evocative function that the word 'God' actually plays in our lives. It raises the question of the origin of reality and calls the whole of existence into question. It points us not to particular experiences but to the enabling condition of all experience. This word is in reality not our own creation, but it creates us and our history. Its very existence in our culture, even when used by atheists, is a reminder that we cannot ultimately evade the mystery implied in our experience. In short, the very word 'God' has a mystagogical power.

In summary, the mystagogue does not have to avoid conceptually precise language but can fruitfully employ it in an evocative way along with poetic descriptions to disclose and articulate the mystery dimension of experience.

3. Mystagogy should make use of a phenomenological method in order to investigate self-experience for intimations of mystery. In general this means that the task of the mystagogue is to describe significant aspects of human experience carefully and accurately, avoiding distortions, hasty interpretations, and all types of reductionism. A good phenomenology will stay open to the full range of experience trying to disclose the dimension of mystery which often lies hidden in human existence. The rationale for this approach is found in a proper anthropology. If it is true that human beings are essentially and necessarily oriented to gracious mystery, then the deeper and more precise our descriptions of common human experience, the more likely they are to disclose this fundamental orientation which grounds all human activity. In other words, accurate descriptions of our transcendentality are going to reveal an infinite horizon which can be properly named "God."

In working out a proper and helpful phenomenology we could concentrate, as did Husserl, on man's conscious ego attempting to describe man's cognitive consciousness and its intentionality toward the infinite.[17] We could broaden the descriptions beyond cognitive consciousness to include affective states and everyday life in the world. This would come closer to the type of existential phenomenology practiced by Heidegger in *Being and Time*, which concentrates on manifesting the hidden aspects of man's being in the world.[18] Finally, it would be helpful to be more conscious of the symbolic character of self-experience, or, more precisely, the way in which symbols affect self-interpretation. We find an example of this approach in Paul Ricoeur, who stresses the importance of investigating the symbolic and linguistic dimension of human existence.[19] Whatever the precise form, phenomenology, broadly conceived as careful description of common human experience, is one of the major tools of the mystagogue as I will try to illustrate in the second part of this book.

4. It is helpful to consider mystagogy as the "wooing of an elite."[20] It should quickly be pointed out that the term 'elite' does not refer to any socioeconomic class nor does it indicate superior intelligence or academic attainments. The elite in question are those who have an ability to reflect on and verbalize religious experience, a capability which seems to be reserved to a relative few in contemporary society and which can be understood as analogous to having an ear for music. In other words, because the sociological support for theism has been diminished, many people today seem to be incapable of achieving an explicit religious self-interpretation. According to this analysis secular atheists are precisely those who have not reached the stage of being able to attain a comprehensive view of their lives or who cannot objectify such a religious view in conceptual terms. It seems that pastoral experience corroborates this analysis and that theology can help interpret it. Briefly, the grace of salvation is offered to all persons and will be fruitful if not thwarted by serious, enduring, sinful culpability; the grace of reflective awareness of this situation is given only to some as a sign of the universal, salvific, self-communication of God.[21] If mystagogues take this analysis seriously, it will affect their outlook and practice.

(a) They will consider their own theistic position to be more enlightened than that of the atheist who has not yet achieved such a complete self-understanding. "This attitude," writes Rahner, "in which theism justifiably feels itself superior to this kind of atheism, should come to be accepted as obvious. The theist should no longer feel himself to be the one who is defending an old theory against a modern viewpoint, but rather as the one who humanly speaking and in the concrete conditions of human living, has advanced farther than the atheist."[22] The advantage of this outlook is that it allows Christian mystagogues to be less defensive and enables them to deal more comfortably with the fact that so many do not share their theistic position. They can remind themselves that many who reject their interpretations either do not have the requisite experience or, for very understandable reasons, cannot adequately articulate the full dimension of their self-experience.[23] In brief, seeing mystagogy as wooing an elite helps apologists to achieve a healthy outlook on their ministry and to maintain psychic balance in the midst of many failures.

(b) This approach is in reality a means of maximizing the effectiveness of the mystagogical effort. It has the psychological advantage of presenting theism as a comprehensive viewpoint which is difficult to attain and which demands a dedicated response. In addition, the mystagogue can present it calmly and confidently without defensiveness or subtle coercion. Many today will find such a confident invitation to examine a comprehensive claim more attractive than a watered-down version anxiously presented.

Another aspect of the utility of this approach is that it frees Christian apologists from the tyranny of numbers.[24] There is no need for frenzied effort to convert all those who seem to lack a feel for explicit religion. On the contrary, there is a proper confidence in the universal salvific will of God and in the invisible workings of his grace. In fact, it may prove more effective in the long run to have fewer but more committed believers who have come to a genuine sense of mystery and have accepted the full Christian interpretation of human existence.

While the phrase 'wooing an elite' has questionable overtones and must be preserved from misunderstanding, it is a striking reminder that the contemporary apologist should maintain a confident and intelligently aggressive posture in the midst of an increasingly secularized and atheistic world. Mystagogues will often find that their descriptions and interpretations fall on deaf ears. In these cases they must have a sound theological position that allows them to avoid both the paralysis of despair and a neurotic Messiah complex that forgets that God has already entered where human words are refused.

5. Silent meditation involving self-confrontation is a valuable mystagogical technique. In a busy world inclined toward the eclipse of mystery it is important to find time to quiet the mind and heart and to enter into the mysterious depths of the true self.[25]

Such an effort to encounter the mystery which engulfs our very being is not easy. Let us imagine one way the process might work.[26] We sit down to be quiet with ourselves but find that we are tempted to escape in many ways: through external distractions, imaginary conversations with others, internal dialogue with our self, and so on. If we can overcome these temptations and return to a simple silence, it will allow our deepest feelings to rise to the surface. As they struggle into consciousness, it is important not to explain them away too quickly or draw hasty generalizations. It is better to give them full sway, feel them intensely, and even allow them to take us over. Amidst some clear longings for love, truth, goodness, and the like, there may also appear more negative feelings such as utter aloneness, emptiness, and even self-disgust. If we can endure these feelings, they may grow into a sense of being encompassed by nothingness or of hovering over a void which cannot be escaped. There may be an inclination at this point to name this mysterious reality "God" and to turn to prayer for comfort and consolation. However, on occasion it will be instructive to avoid this familiar practice and instead to face the full ambiguity of these primary feelings. Is the void a cruel fate which brings death and judgment or the gracious mystery which brings happiness and peace? The great comprehensive question of existence is now before us: meaningfulness or absurdity, light or darkness, life or death. We may find that the simple enduring of the dark nothingness will reveal its limits and impotency, and leave us with a peaceful sense of the friendly character of the encompassing mystery and a word of thanks on our lips. It is also possible that the stark ambivalence of the experience will remain dominant in our consciousness and no clear resolution will appear. In either case such a confrontation with self has an authenticity about it and a power to expose the folly of escapism and the shallowness of easy answers. At its best it allows us to sense the presence of the gracious mystery. At the very least it expands our capacity to understand religious interpretation and to appreciate theistic expressions.

Of course, the silent confrontation with self could take many other directions. Whatever its precise form, it remains a valuable mystagogical tool because of its great potential for opening up the mysterious depths of self-experience which are often obscured even for reflective people.

6. Theology should play an important role in the mystagogical enterprise. It is possible to discern three distinct ways in which it can share in the task of disclosing and interpreting the dimension of mystery in human experience.

(a) One of the primary functions of theology itself is to lead people into mystery.[27] This means that it is not merely a conceptual exercise nor analysis of language (even if this is concerned with the absolute mystery) but an initiation into the experience of grace. In other words, theology is not a neutral, objective science but a passionate effort to interpret our grace-filled existence which in turn brings us to a conscious awareness of the mystery ruling our lives. That theology leads to mystery is not a regrettable failure, for genuine theology always points beyond itself to the God who remains ultimately mysterious. This must be made clear to people today lest they think that theology simply speaks poetically about matters that science will one day clarify.

Theology achieves such a mystagogical orientation, not by abandoning its scientific character, but by becoming more rigorously scientific. This means the better job theologians do of posing the proper questions, of critically examining the resources of the Christian tradition, and of struggling to find contemporary formulations, the greater is the chance that their findings will serve the needs of people today. The more they are in touch with the mood of the times, including the mentality of those who experience the "absence of God," the better position they are in to do theology with a mystagogical orientation. In this effort they should see their theological statements not as pictures of reality but as windows from which one views a presence that is beyond all comprehension. The true theologians will remain aware that God is greater than any system and will fight the tendency for theology to become an end in itself.

In all of this, theology is not to be confused with kerygma. It remains a science, which serves mystagogy by being faithful to its own nature as a systematic and rigorous reflection on graced self-experience. However, in this very function theology reveals itself as *initiation into mystery* since it points beyond itself to the source and horizon of all its efforts to illumine human experience.

(b) Theology also serves mystagogy by fighting all reductionist positions which raise a partial aspect of reality into an absolute and present this as the norm for interpreting all experience. In the face of the temptation to make a part of existence into the whole, theology must show that human transcendentality points to an infinite horizon that can never be filled by any finite reality. For example, theologians in dialogue with scientists have the job of indicating the blind spots and limited perspectives in the scientific outlook. They should stress the provisional character of science and point out the temptation of every science to become autonomous and totalitarian. The theologian must be the one who is alert to the element of mystery which can never be analyzed scientifically and which itself holds open the possibility of all scientific progress. In other words, they must raise the deeper questions of the purpose of human existence as a whole, the values which guide human effort, and the very meaning of the scientific enterprise. Their role is, not so much to contribute specific information from their own discipline, but to remind the other participants of the element of mystery which surrounds their particular scientific work.

We could take this example as a model for the general mystagogical function of theology, which is to criticize all reductionist tendencies, thereby creating a climate where many disciplines can contribute to our understanding of the depth and richness of human existence without pretending to exhaust its mystery.

(c) However, it is not enough for theology simply to demonstrate in an abstract way that self-experience implies the presence of mystery. It must also point out the particular concrete ways in which people today encounter this mystery.

If the experience of self is the experience of God, then it seems that a more precise picture of this relationship could be worked out.[28] For example, a loss of personal identity would involve a loss of the sense of God, while a trusting self-acceptance would necessarily imply an acceptance of God. In this fashion it would be theoretically possible to chart the whole history of an individual's self-development and to relate this to an evolving relationship to God. This would allow us to show exactly where religious language fits on the map of human experience.

If it is true that certain types of experience today have a greater power to bring the mystery dimension of life to conscious awareness, then we ought to be able to isolate, describe, and interpret them. For example, we could describe and analyze the modern experience of the burden of freedom in a way which would open up the question of an ultimate source of this aspect of human self-transcendence. It would also be possible to supplement this exercise in transcendental mystagogy with an effort to link this analysis of freedom with the Christian understanding of God who calls on human beings to create and shape the world.

In general, it seems that theology could serve mystagogy by indicating and analyzing particular human experiences which are existentially significant and have a special power to overcome the eclipse of mystery which impoverishes many people today.[29] In Chapter Seven I will attempt to implement this notion by proposing two models of mystery which illumine and thematize the dimension of mystery in our questioning and our freedom.

CHAPTER FIVE

Mystagogy Defended

I HAVE BEEN USING seminal ideas of Karl Rahner in establishing a formal framework for the initial steps of a contemporary apologetics. In order to put the whole project on solid ground it is necessary to respond to certain objections which call into question the general adequacy of his thought for our purposes.

1. Some would immediately deny Rahner's relevance for the mystogogical task because they consider him to be merely a "Denzinger theologian" whose whole theology is built upon defending and interpreting Church dogmas.[1] However, his continuous interest in religious experience and his extensive efforts to uncover the dimension of mystery in ordinary human existence certainly belie the picture of a "house theologian" engaged full time in subtle scholastic distinctions. Strikingly, we find that before the publication of his initial philosophical works, *Geist in Welt* and *Hörer des Wortes* in 1939 and 1941 respectively, he had already written a number of theological articles dealing with religious experience. It is striking because commentators almost universally begin their discussion of Rahner with his philosophical works and the influence of Maréchal and Heidegger.[2] As a matter of fact, decisive and lifelong spiritual influences can be discerned in the works of the early Rahner. His interest in religious experience is not confined to a later period, as even a sketchy review of his early writings would show.[3] Although many seem to think of him only in terms of the reinterpretation of doctrine and as a bridge between a traditional scholasticism and the modern world, our selective reading of his material has revealed a consistent anthropocentric approach and a continuing interest in religious experience which I believe can effectively guide the Christian apologist in the decades ahead.

2. There have been severe criticisms of the anthropocentric approach taken by Rahner.[4] The essence of these objections is that he is in danger of some sort of reductionism: making Christianity

48

into a mere humanism, forcing the scriptures to fit his philosophical concepts, leaving out important aspects of revelation that do not fit his system, or constricting the divine reality within human limits.

First of all, it must be admitted and highlighted that Rahner's work does contain a radically anthropocentric methodology. This is already clear in *Spirit in the World* where he works out a metaphysics of knowledge based on Thomistic principles but in the perspective of the Kantian Copernican revolution.[5] The human knower as a dynamic questioner is clearly in the center of the analysis. The process of knowing is not a matter of analyzing a world out there but is primarily a matter of an enriched self-presence or self-modification. The world is known not as an objective phenomenon but as the reflection of the human spirit which in turn is intentionally present to the knower. God is known not as an infinite being deduced from the physical world but as the condition which makes all human knowing possible.

In this approach human existence is the paradigmatic instance of created being, and therefore the principle object of philosophical reflection.[6] In this regard Rahner states that "for human beings the ontologically first and fundamental case or paradigm of a being and of its fundamental properties is found in the being himself who knows and acts."[7] Thus we come to know what is meant by the basic metaphysical realities such as being, truth, goodness, mystery, by reflecting on our own human operations. Our knowing process should not be considered as mere conceptualization confined to an ideal order and set apart from the real world of physical objects. On the contrary, we are most in touch with the nature of reality by appropriating our own spiritual acts of knowing and willing. In this perspective, metaphysics is properly an analysis of the human existent because the question about being and its universal and necessary properties forms an essential unity with the question about the nature of human existence.[8]

When Rahner turns to the philosophy of religion in *Hearers of the Word*, his fundamental insight developed in his philosophy of knowing leads him to reject the search for an external objective revelation and to adopt an anthropocentric approach in which persons are seen as free finite spirits listening in their history for a possible word from the Lord. A contemporary philosophy of religion must be based on an analysis of human beings as open to and desirous of a fulfilling word.

This radical anthropocentrism is carried over into Rahner's theological method since for him "dogmatic theology today must be theological anthropology."[9] The study of human beings is not a separate realm of inquiry distinct from properly theological topics but is itself the whole of theology. This means that we only know about God by knowing about ourselves. It is by investigating human experience in all its depth that we come to know the significance of particular Christian doctrines. Thus, even this brief treatment suggests that there is in Rahner's work an anthropocentric approach which is strikingly radical and comprehensive.[10]

In defending this method we should first note that Rahner sees himself as continuing the anthropocentrism already begun in Aquinas. He has judged it important to maintain the dialogue with modern philosophy since Descartes and Kant and to align himself with the pioneering work of Blondel, Rousselot, and Maréchal in challenging the narrowness of modern subjectivism.

This can be accomplished, not by totally rejecting the turn to the personal subject, but by insisting that human beings are, in all aspects and dimensions of their existence, referred to the absolute mystery which we call God. Reductionism, or "mere humanism," results, not from beginning with human beings, but from not probing deeply enough into human experience and from truncating the truly human.

The major point to be emphasized in this regard is that persons are, not self-centered autonomous individuals, but creatures whose essence is to be open to the absolute. Our very nature already involves us in a relation to God. It is a question, not of finding a place for a transcendent realm after viewing human beings in a purely natural way, but of remembering that concrete persons are always, from the very beginning, immersed in a world of mystery. For Rahner this anthropology is not merely a theoretical starting point to be abandoned in later humanistic speculation or reductionist reinterpretations of Christian doctrines. It is the continually revived inspiration for a vast amount of theological reflection that leads back to the incomprehensible mystery we call "God." His fundamental understanding of persons as always already oriented to the gracious mystery is like a powerful searchlight which he has used to illumine all the theological issues presented to him by the contemporary world.[11] It has allowed him to dialogue effectively with nonbelievers, to produce an organic and consistent theology, and to reinterpret Christian doctrines in contemporary language.

In view of both the starting point and its practical application the charge of reductionism seems to lack much force. In fact, it seems to me that the Rahnerian approach is uniquely qualified to counter modern efforts to imprison people in their finitude, precisely because it concentrates on revealing a dimension of mystery in the kind of ordinary human experience accessible to all.

There is a further advantage in his methodology. It is a matter, not simply of beginning with human existence as the paradigm, but of insisting on the need for individuals to appropriate their own spiritual functions.[12] This means that we must become more aware of the distinctive ways in which throughout our lives we have personally encountered and responded to the mystery that surrounds us. This whole line of thought has obvious implications for a mystagogy concerned with disclosing a sense of mystery. It provides us with a sound theoretical basis for the currently popular story or narrative theology.[13] In other words, a totally anthropocentric approach leads to an interest not just in human beings in general but to one's own experience. The question is not simply what is man, but who am I.[14]

3. Another set of criticisms can be summarized under the notion that Rahner's approach is too individualistic. In this regard Johannes Metz, surely a friendly critic, writes:

> Is there not danger that the question of salvation will be made too private and that salvation history will be conceived too worldlessly, breaking too quickly the point of the universal historical battle for man?[15]

His point is that political, social, institutional, and eschatalogical elements are in danger of being neglected in Rahner's theology since it centers on the individual subject as oriented toward the absolute mystery. This criticism was developed by Eberhard Simons,[16] who (basing himself on only one work, *Hörer des Wortes*) argues that Rahner's metaphysics concentrates too much on abstract objective knowledge, misses the dialogic character of human existence, and therefore cannot properly ground the interpersonal dimension of life.[17] Alexander Gerken has taken this critique and applied it to Rahner's theology by claiming that he is not open to the interpersonal aspects of revelation.[18] In the same general vein, Shubert Ogden claims that Rahner's notion of knowledge as self-possession, with its emphasis on individual subjectivity, fails to give him adequate conceptual tools for interpreting human existence. Ogden argues that if we view knowledge as possession of the other, we are in a better position to understand the social and relational character of reality.[19] The essence of these criticisms is that Rahner's starting point is too narrow and is not open to the communal, social, and political aspects of human experience. This objection is extremely important from the viewpoint of our project, since it is vital that we have a framework for our analysis which is open to the whole range of human experience. Furthermore, since interpersonal relationships are highly esteemed by many today as a valuable source of insight into human life, it is especially important that the interpersonal dimension not be excluded a priori.

Rahner himself has recognized this objection and suggested a twofold response: he should not be judged simply by his early works *Geist in Welt* and *Hörer des Wortes,* and he has produced a very abstract and formal framework which remains open to further clarification, especially in terms of historicity and interpersonal relations.[20] The first point is well taken. So often critics (Simons is a good example here) have taken a single work of Rahner and used it to make a case against his thought as a whole, while they fail to note that he has provided the counterpoint elsewhere. Let us look more closely at the second part of his response. I think Rahner is correct in saying that his system is open to the social and communal dimensions. For him a person's transcendental relationship to being in general can be mediated by any and all human experience. To express this theologically, we can say that all things are potentially revelatory. In terms of mystagogy any finite reality can be the catalyst for a movement from transcendental to categorical awareness. Therefore, in principle both the institutional and the interpersonal can be said to be within the framework of his analysis from the very beginning. Furthermore, among the various mediating elements some seem to have a greater power to force us to confront ourselves and to open up the dimension of mystery. Clearly, for Rahner, personal relationships have this power to a preeminent degree.[21] However, there is a still more radical response to the charge of being closed to the interpersonal. Rahner writes:

> Yet since knowledge (being itself already an act) attains its proper and full nature only in the act of freedom and therefore must lose and yet keep itself in freedom in order to be completely itself, it has a fully human significance only once it is integrated into freedom, i.e. into the loving communication with the Thou. The act of personal love for another human being is therefore the all-embracing basic act of man which gives meaning, direction and measure to everything else. If this is correct, then the essential *a priori* openness to the other human being which must be undertaken freely belongs as such to the *a priori* and most basic constitution of man and is an essential inner

moment of his (knowing and willing) transcendentality. *This a priori* basic constitution (which must be accepted in freedom, but to which man can also close himself) is experienced in the concrete encounter with man in the concrete. The moral (or immoral) basic act in which man comes to himself and decides basically about himself is also the (loving or hating) communication with the concrete Thou in which man experiences, accepts or denies his basic *a priori* reference to the Thou as such.[22]

Here, personal relationships are not just one of many mediating factors but are demanded by the very essence of human beings. Our knowledge and freedom are enacted precisely through the encounter with another person. We find and fulfill ourselves in a personal environment. Rahner has rooted the interpersonal in the essential structures of human nature and thus counters any suggestion that his starting point has imprisoned him in a private, individualistic anthropology with no opening to the social and communal dimensions of life.[23]

While the pure openness to the interpersonal is clearly established, it seems to me that Rahner has never really integrated it into his own theological psyche.[24] His instincts are still with the private and the individualistic, rather than the social and the communal. He has described himself as basically a nineteenth-century individualist. When faced with a new theological problem, his tendency is to search for an ultimate solution in terms of the individual's relation to the mystery. Even in his recent works he still employs the individualistic conceptual scheme taken from his metaphysics of knowledge in order to explain human transcendentality. He has, on occasion, manifested a certain discomfort with Metz's political theology, claiming he was not sure he understood it properly. Taken together, these points indicate that Rahner's theological instincts are more individualistic than communal. However, even this assessment must be balanced by a number of other factors: he has written widely and impressively on social and institutional themes; he has argued persuasively for the establishment of a discipline called "practical theology" which would analyze society from a theological perspective; he has been an important contributor to the Christian-Marxist dialogue; he has tried to integrate political and social themes into his transcendental method. It would surely be a mistake to say that Rahner's initial, admittedly individualistic, insight has prevented him from contributing to the discussion of social and institutional questions. Putting all these considerations together, I would summarize my own position in this way: although Rahner's deepest instincts remain individualistic, his fundamental theological approach is definitely open to the interpersonal and institutional dimensions of human existence, and thus has enabled him to make important contributions to social questions.[25]

4. Another objection that is significant for our purposes is that Rahner is not consistent on the question of the relationship between nature and grace. This general problem has elicited a great deal of comment,[26] but the point that concerns us is best expressed by William Shepherd:

> When Rahner attempts to deal with the technical problem of nature and grace, he moves out of the theological framework of thought which is a characteristic and necessary context for the development of his system of doctrines. He reverts to the loci pattern of post-Tridentine scholastic theology, and, in addition, he accepts its fundamental view of the world instead of his own modern one. The world-order envisaged by classical Roman Catholic theology becomes the framework for his resolution of the technical problem of nature and grace, and the unified, evolutionary picture of the world which underlies his whole theological system recedes into the background. An equivocation between his theological system and his technical doctrine of nature and grace consequently occurs; it is rendered all the more serious because his theological system as a whole must be construed as 'theology of nature and grace'.[27]

I think Shepherd has isolated a real problem and correctly assessed its significance. We could restate the difficulty: although according to his total theological vision persons are concrete unified beings who have always existed in a supernatural order, Rahner sometimes speaks as though individuals were a combination of nature and supernature who, on occasion, function in a purely natural way.[28] Shepherd explains the inconsistency in this way: Rahner has written his technical articles on nature and grace within the traditional static framework of scholastic debates—trying to defend the gratuity of grace and at the same time avoid seeing it in terms of an extrinsic superstructure. In this context he views man as a being composed of pure nature which does not in itself have a necessary ordination to the divine, along with a supernatural existential which does give man such an orientation. In addition, Rahner's language sometimes suggests that man existed as pure nature and was at some particular time elevated to a higher state.[29] However, when Rahner operates within his more familiar evolutionary world view, he sees man clearly as a concrete unified whole existing from the beginning within a created order oriented toward God.[30] While this explanation is helpful, it does not explain this inconsistency when it appears outside of the technical debate over the nature-grace relationship. In other words, the problem antedates Rahner's entrance into this controversy in 1950.[31]

The simpler and more comprehensive explanation is that Rahner only gradually came to see that the concrete nature of every human being is always already conditioned by the offer of God's grace. It is not that he denied this thesis, but it was simply not operative in much of his early writing. Gradually the more positive understanding of the universal salvific will of God came to dominate his thinking and was reflected in his outlook on concrete human nature. Given this explanation, my approach to appropriating Rahner for the apologetic task is to bypass both the technical discussion of the nature-grace problematic and the imprecise language which suggests a purely natural human experience and, instead, to employ his more developed statements which presume that human beings in their actual existence are always conditioned by grace. I think the charge of inconsistency is best resolved by admitting the early imprecision and allowing for an evolution in Rahner's understanding of the ramifications of his own fundamental insights.

5. Langdon Gilkey, in reviewing *Spirit in the World*,[32] makes a sharp attack on the way Rahner has worked out his fundamental philosophical position. He levels these charges: Rahner offers no phenomenological, linguistic, or speculative analyses of knowing; he makes no references to other contemporary psychologists or philosophers who have studied the same topic; he proves his points only by showing they are genuinely Thomistic. This leads Gilkey to state: "The method Rahner employs here seems to have no legitimate usage in answering the relevant philosophical question: What is man?"[33] Although Gilkey is commenting on only one book, his criticism is important because it attacks the way that Rahner arrived at the philosophical formulation of the fundamental insight that inspires all his work.

In responding we should first recall the context in which Rahner was writing. It is my opinion that he had already achieved in his early writings on spirituality an understanding of human existence as essentially open to the incomprehensible mystery and was attempting in *Spirit in the World* to ground this in a metaphysics of knowledge. In addition, he was forced by circumstances to write a Thomistic-inspired thesis, which explains the constant references to Aquinas.[34] Second, it is not true that *Spirit in the World* contains no phenomenology or systematic treatment of human knowing.[35] While many long passages do seem to be merely proof texts from Aquinas, there are significant contributions of Rahner himself:[36] a descriptive analysis of human questioning (pp. 57–65), a systematic presentation of the unity of being and knowing (pp. 67–77), an original contribution to the topic which shows abstraction and conversion to the phantasm to be two sides of the one knowing process (pp. 117–120),[37] the development of the notion of human transcendence and its infinite goal (pp. 142–145), an attempt to meet the objections of Kant and Heidegger and to establish the existence of an infinite horizon (pp. 146–163, 169–173, 183–187), introduction of the distinction between unobjective and objective consciousness (p. 182), establishment of the key idea that "intellectual knowledge is possible only with a simultaneous realization of sense knowledge" (p. 237), the idea that finite spirit necessarily produces bodiliness and sensibility (pp. 284–286), and, finally, an important discussion of the possibility of metaphysics, even though all knowledge involves imaginative elements (pp. 387–408).

The point of this brief review is to respond to Gilkey by indicating that indeed a systematic metaphysics of knowledge with a distinctively Rahnerian cast (with dependence on Maréchal and Heidegger, of course) can be distilled from a work admittedly heavy-laden with attempts to be Thomistic. When we combine this material with insights from *Hearers of the Word, Hominisation,* and other sources, it seems to me that we have a well-founded original contribution to a metaphysics of knowledge which creatively combines Thomistic, Heideggerian, and Maréchalian elements.[38]

6. We should also note the critique of Rahner's fundamental approach to the metaphysics of knowledge which comes from the more traditional Thomists.[39] The essence of this objection is that Rahner puts too much emphasis on the subjective input in the knowing process and thereby undercuts the Thomistic principle that all knowledge comes through the senses. He has accepted Kant too uncritically in adopting the transcendental method. The critics want all metaphysical knowledge to be deduced by reasoning from sense experience and not to be derived in part from the agent intellect, as Rahner would have it. As Maritain says concerning metaphysical realities such as uncreated Being: "It is by a reasoning process starting from the data which are given us by the facts of sensible existence that we are able to know them."[40] For Etienne Gilson, another great representative of neo-Thomism, there can be no innate knowledge, no a priori input, and, strictly speaking, no deduction of metaphysical re-

alities. On the contrary, we know the existence of everything, even being itself, in an a posteriori fashion, that is, by perceiving it.[41] The significance of this neo-Thomistic critique is that it calls into question the whole transcendental method (based on the discovery of the a priori conditions which make knowing possible) employed by Rahner in all his anthropocentric philosophy and theology and thereby challenges much of his mystagogically oriented material.

There are a number of ways of responding to this criticism. We could point to the exciting and fruitful accomplishments of authors such as Maréchal, Lotz, Lonergan, and Coreth who have employed this method.[42] It could be argued that Rahner's method is authentically Thomistic, since Aquinas clearly recognized an a priori element in the knowing process, especially in his teaching on the light of the agent intellect and the way we know first principles.[43] It could be maintained that a method which emphasizes subjective factors has a better chance of getting a hearing in the modern world than the classical cosmocentrism of the neo-Thomists. It is also possible to mount a philosophical critique of the dogmatic empiricism of the neo-Thomists on the grounds that it is not legitimate to arrive at metaphysical certitude based solely on sense experience which always remains contingent. In addition, there can be worked out a philosophical defense of the transcendental method based on the fact that sense experience is in itself only potentially intelligible and that it requires some active agent (the agent intellect within the knower) to make it actually intelligible.[44]

However, without developing these various approaches, I think that the most effective response for our purposes is suggested by Rahner's own explanation of transcendental method.[45] He recognizes the problem in determining the technical meaning of transcendental philosophy and in establishing a precise and consistent notion of it which would be beyond dispute. Without limiting himself to historical developments since Descartes or Kant, he assumes a wider notion of "transcendental method" and claims that all metaphysics and all genuine theology have always employed this approach. His interest here is to find a solid basis for his own method which is not dependent on any one philosophical school of thought. He does not want his theological system to rise or fall with philosophical trends.[46] Therefore, he tries to base his approach on a popular, prephilosophical understanding of a transcendental method which is in no way dependent on the general consensus of philosophers. For him a transcendental approach simply means that the question of the conditions in the knower which make human knowing possible is taken seriously.[47]

Actually, it seems obvious that in all knowing both the object known and the knower are involved. Objects are never known in some chemically pure way, since the subjective input of the knower always colors the total understanding of the object.[48] The older scientific ideal of a totally neutral, objective analysis of natural phenomenon has given way to a realization that the observer always influences the act of observing itself. Common sense tells us that we filter knowledge through our subjective disposition: our interest and cares help determine our perceptions, our alertness and training are factors in gaining insight, our personalities and cultural conditioning influence our judgments. Such subjective factors are not just one element among many in the knowing process but are part of the a priori conditions of all knowing, and therefore they have a special significance.[49]

If it is once admitted that there is a significant subjective input involved in the knowing process, then it seems clearly legitimate, and even necessary, to try to discover and thematize this factor. This is what Rahner means by transcendental inquiry, and it is the method he has used in his own mystagogically oriented theology. There may be arguments about how to carry out this transcendental analysis, but it seems to me that the fundamental validity of the method has been established.

7. It is sometimes suggested that Rahner's thought is passé, that his day is over, and that his work is not particularly helpful for meeting contemporary challenges. I would like to argue that, on the contrary, his work contains uniquely helpful resources for responding to the current problem of the eclipse of mystery. In support of the contemporary relevance of Rahner's thought in general we might note the comment of John Macquarrie:

> Among contemporary theologians, I have found Karl Rahner the most helpful. In saying this, I am acknowledging that the leadership in theology, which even ten years ago lay with such Protestant giants as Barth, Brunner, and Tillich, has now passed to Roman Catholic thinkers. Among them, Karl Rahner (himself a penetrating student of Heidegger) is outstanding. He handles in a masterly way those tensions which constitute the peculiar dialectic of theology mentioned above: faith and reason, tradition and novelty, authority and freedom, and so on.[50]

When we turn to the specific question of apologetics, I see a number of advantages of Rahner's thought over other possibilities: his thoroughly anthropocentric approach has a better chance of getting a hearing from secularized people than any of the neo-orthodox theologies (including Hans Küng and the European theologians of hope) which work primarily from biblical categories; his somber mood and realistic outlook are more believable to a sceptical generation than the optimistic view of Teilhard de Chardin (in addition, Rahner's comprehensive theological system seems to have a staying power not matched by Teilhard's individual, if brilliant, insights which never flowered into a complete theology); his extensive and developed treatment of all the major theological themes puts Rahner in a better position to carry out the complete apologetic task than the process theologians who have not yet achieved a detailed theological system; his emphasis on the fact that the divine manifests itself in the whole range of experience of all people is more appealing to contemporary persons than the more restricted view of revelation offered by Tillich (although the latter's work does offer great resources for the mystagogical task, as witnessed by Gilkey's use of it); finally, Rahner's notion of the transcendent as mystery will prove more helpful than Lonergan's understanding of transcendence.

The last point can stand further development since it brings out one of the fundamental reasons why Rahner's thought is particularly well suited for the mystagogical task. For Lonergan an analysis of man's cognitional process reveals him to be a self-transcendent knower. He is characterized by the desire to know, an inquiring spirit that is never totally satisfied by any particular answers.[51] Therefore, the only possible objective of this dynamism is being itself, which is characterized as "all that is known and all that remains to be known" and as that which is "known by the totality of true judgments."[52] Without going into other aspects of Lonergan's position, we can say that for him the emphasis is on being as that which is to be known. In contrast, Rahner views the object of human transcendentality precisely as that which is not known. It is the ever-receding horizon, the unfathomable source, the infinite which is always greater than our grasp. "Being" as the object of human striving is fundamentally incomprehensible. It is, in a word, mystery.

Lonergan himself has highlighted this difference in his well-known remark: "Rahner emphasizes mystery a lot. I have a few clear things to say."[53] I think it is precisely this emphasis on mystery which makes Rahner's thought so valuable for an age that is in danger of viewing human existence on the model of a sophisticated computer. Rationalism cannot be fought by rationalistic approaches. Scientism is not overcome by the addition of a little bit of mystery after science reaches its limits. The strength of Rahner is that the mystery dimension appears at the very beginning of his analysis and is seen as the ever-incomprehensible horizon for all of human activity. Mystery is clearly not something to be overcome by science, but functions as an ever-present invitation for us to transcend ourselves. This Rahnerian insight seems to me to be exactly what is needed in dealing with those who suffer from an eclipse of mystery.

In addition, it is my opinion that Rahner provides us with the most convincing and radical critique of the pipeline tendencies (as described in Chapter One) found among some Christians today. In his metaphysics of knowledge he has demonstrated that a direct and immediate apprehension of being (or God) is impossible for the human knower.[54] Human beings are finite spirits who begin their questioning immersed in a world of matter and come to the knowledge of universal essences by abstracting from concrete singulars. This suggests that bodiliness is an essential aspect of the finite spirit, the human spirit is dependent on the senses, sense intuition is always the basis for thought, intellectual intuition is impossible, there is no concept without image, there is no thinking without imagination. This means that metaphysical realities (God, being, the mystery) can only be co-known in the knowing of particular finite realities and can never be directly and immediately comprehended. They are known as the light in which our knowing of particular objects takes place, as the condition of possibility for knowing the universal essences of finite realities.[55]

This fundamental insight into the nature of human knowing has been applied by Rahner to his theology as well. He has insisted that any self-communication of God will come to human beings in their concrete history. It is the very particular experience of self, as we have seen, which is the experience of God. Interaction with other persons is a major catalyst for bringing the divine presence to mind. There is no abstract love of God apart from love of neighbor. God is to be found in the ordinary and the everyday. There is no imageless mysticism which escapes from the common structure of faith that always involves surrender to a God who remains incomprehensible.[56] Christianity is not a timeless, abstract philosophy of life but an acceptance of the scandalous particularity that God has revealed himself most completely in the Jewish male Jesus of Nazareth. Ontologism in all its forms is to be rejected because the goal of human transcendentality is never experienced in itself but is only known unobjectively in the experience of self-transcendence.[57] In developing all of these themes at length Rahner has remained true to his basic insight that God is known never directly and immediately but always indirectly as the incomprehensible goal of an always ambiguous human experience.

In summary, from both a philosophical and theological viewpoint Rahner provides us with a radical critique of pipeline Christianity, one which undercuts all pretensions to a direct, immediate, unambiguous apprehension of the mystery in rule over our lives.

In trying to establish Rahner's relevance for contemporary apologetics we should recall here the point he made in the Introduction to this book about his limited contribution to the question of mystagogy. After mentioning various mystagogical techniques in a 1974 letter to Klaus Fischer, he expressed this limitation very explicitly:

> About this side of a comprehensive mystagogy I have really never spoken, without thereby suggesting that it is unimportant for the Christian life. However, even the truly Christian and theological side of mystagogy has been expressed by me only as a theme and a demand. I have nowhere stated many detailed, clear, or practical ideas on the topic. This lack is to be honestly admitted.[58]

Despite this disclaimer, I still contend that Rahner's philosophical and theological works provide us with the most helpful resources for constructing a viable mystagogy. It is true that he has not thematized the material, but the elements are there: recognition of the dimensions and depth of the problem; powerful insights into human nature and the human situation; the important and consistently applied distinction between the transcendental and categorical dimension of experience; numerous methodological suggestions which can be applied to the problem; helpful explanations of the category "self-experience"; realistic, and at times poetic, descriptions of human experience; and, especially, a consistent and comprehensive theological system. Rahner often produces more than his disclaimers suggest.

Of course, the material we have used from Rahner in constructing the framework for a mystagogical program could be enriched by additions from other traditions or authors. His notion of experience, which he developed primarily under the heading of "self-experience," could be filled out still further by the American pragmatic tradition, where "experience" is the basic category.[59] Rahner's very helpful distinction between transcendental and categorical consciousness could be further specified through the detailed analysis of Bernard Lonergan which distinguishes thirty-one different types of differentiated consciousness.[60] As we have previously noted, Rahner's individualistic starting point could be supplemented by a more interpersonal approach which would be based on a phenomenology of the encounter between persons and a metaphysical analysis of this I-thou relationship.[61] Important additions to his methodological suggestions could be gathered from the Eastern religious traditions with their great stress on the concrete techniques for achieving greater self-awareness and enlightenment.[62] In addition, the analytic tradition could aid us in appropriating Rahner's ideas.[63] It reminds us of the need to strive for a precise and consistent use of words—a significant point as we recall Rahner's ambiguous use of 'transcendence' and 'transcendental'. It suggests the need for a more critical examination of the role and content of the language used in expressing the a priori conditions uncovered by Rahner's transcendental analyses.[64] We find in this tradition helpful alternative formulations of the problem of the eclipse of mystery and of the mystagogical task. For example, it can be asked whether religious language is meaningful and how it can be used to map the depths of human experience. Finally, some authors have suggested that an analysis of language can open up the dimensions of mystery without the Rahnerian talk of incomprehensibility getting swallowed up in meaninglessness.[65] While Rahner's thought is organic and comprehensive, I believe it remains open and can benefit from dialogue with other systems and approaches.

One reason some question Rahner's contemporary usefulness is the abstruse character of his terminology. I am, of course, of the opinion that his insights developed in the context of German intellectual life are applicable to the American scene. In addition, we should remember that he has chosen his terminology carefully (often trying to relate it to traditional usage) and that changing it runs the risk of oversimplification. However, it is clear that we must find a more intelligible vocabulary if we are to retrieve effectively Rahner's ideas for dealing with current problems. For example, 'mystagogy' could be changed to 'consciousness-raising' or 'increasing religious self-awareness', 'transcendental realm' to 'depth dimension', 'categorical' to 'explicit', 'transcendentality' to 'spiritual dynamism', 'transcendental revelation' to 'universal revelation', 'transcendental awareness' to 'mood'.

Despite the objections and limitations I am convinced that Rahner provides us with most helpful resources for constructing an effective apologetic response to the eclipse of mystery. With the framework solidly established, we turn now to the particular task of finding a concrete way of carrying out a transcendental mystagogy, that is, of achieving an increased self-awareness and a more accurate articulation of the depth dimension of common human experience.

PART TWO

CHAPTER SIX

Models of Mystery Explained

AFTER SETTING THE framework, I want to make a substantive contribution to the mystagogical work of the apologist by presenting two "models of mystery": one dealing with human questioning and the other with human freedom. Let me explain what I have in mind.

I. THE PROJECT

The models are primarily a contribution to transcendental mystagogy since they include descriptions and analyses of human experience which are designed to disclose and thematize the dimension of mystery. In a very limited way they involve a categorical mystagogy since they attempt to link experience and one essential Christian doctrine: the existence of the gracious mystery we call "God." From another viewpoint, these models could form the first step in a revised fundamental theology (which has the job of laying the foundations for systematic theology) since they manifest persons as beings who are capable of hearing a possible revelation from God and they illumine particular areas of experience which could be related to individual Christian doctrines.

We can further clarify this project by relating it to some other similar efforts. The closest parallel is Langdon Gilkey's "prolegomenon" to theology, in which he tries to demonstrate the meaningfulness and necessity of religious language even for modern secular man.[1] He does this by a phenomenological analysis of various aspects of human experience showing how they necessarily involve the dimension of what he calls "ultimacy." I discern three main features of Gilkey's work which correspond to what I intend to do: he deals with common human experience rather than explicit religious experience; he makes use of a descriptive method designed to disclose and thematize what is often hidden, repressed, or denied; and he attempts to show that a transcendent dimension is present in particular areas of our experience. There is also a major difference. For Gilkey the question of the validity of his disclosure of ultimacy arises only when it is interpreted in a particular fashion. For example, a truth claim first becomes an issue when Christians interpret the source of ultimacy as the "loving Father."[2] In other words, he offers no metaphysical justification for his original claim that ultimacy is present in human experience. In verifying the Christian interpretation of ultimacy he again leaves no room for philosophical analysis; rather, he bases the verification entirely on the life of the Christian community which is founded on the special revelation of Jesus Christ.[3] In contrast, I will include a philosophical validation of the claim that mystery is necessarily present in human experience. It seems to me that the question of the validity of the disclosure of a transcendent dimension naturally arises even before it is interpreted in a particular way. The normal response to the disclosure of mystery in experience is to understand it as a claim to truth that requires validation. If this is the case, then an effective mystagogy cannot rely simply on phenomenology to disclose the transcendent but must include a vindication of this assertion.

While David Tracy's *Blessed Rage for Order* is a more ambitious undertaking than I have in mind, there are aspects of his work that correspond to the material in the following chapters. In general he attempts to work out a revised fundamental theology which successively shows that religious, theistic, and christological interpretations of human experience are both meaningful and true.[4] To accomplish this he includes descriptions of common human experience designed to disclose a religious dimension which he describes in terms of "limit questions and situations." While his phenomenology of human experience is very brief, Tracy's insistence on the role of metaphysics in validating the truth claims involved in his interpretation of this experience is more in accord with my approach.

The models also have certain elements in common with John Macquarrie's philosophical theology which begins with man's ordinary experience of himself and attempts both to discern the ontological structures of human existence and to describe man's actual situation in secular terms as a basis for showing the meaningfulness of religious discourse.[5] His clearly anthropocentric approach, his willingness to talk about ontological structures and patterns in human existence, and his recognition of the need to deal with both the existential and ontological aspects of the truth claims of the religious interpretation of life are all points that find parallels in my presentation.[6]

With these comparisons in mind we can summarize the project as the construction and validation of models which, through a descriptive method, disclose the dimension of mystery in common human experience.

II. THE PURPOSE AND STRUCTURE OF THE MODELS

1. We will understand the word 'model' in the very general sense suggested by Bernard Lonergan's statement:

> For models purport to be, not descriptions of reality, not hypotheses about reality, but simply interlocking sets of terms and relations. Such sets, in fact, turn out to be useful in guiding investigations, in framing hypotheses, and in writing descriptions.[7]

He goes on to remind us that models are not something to be imitated, but serve rather to focus attention in a particular direction. For my purposes there are a number of attractive features in this understanding of model: the recognition that reality is greater than any particular objectification of it, the perception that models are clearly not pictures of reality but are designed to direct attention in specific ways, the appreciation that models are composed of various elements which must be properly related in order to function effectively. Thus, Lonergan's notion of "model" suggests that we must determine the most effective combination of elements which can best direct attention to the deeper aspects of human experience, while we always remember that experience is never exhausted by our attempt to represent it.

The word 'mystery' specifies the function of these models, which, in general, is to disclose and thematize the transcendent dimension of human experience. In terms of the distinction already established between transcendental and categorical mystagogy, we could say that their function is to arouse the sense of mystery which is often hidden or repressed in modern man and to relate the consciousness of this religious dimension to an explicitly theistic interpretation. This distinction is similar to the one employed by Ewert Cousins between "experiential models" which attempt to bring to light the hidden riches of personal religious experience and "expressive models" which thematize the various available objectifications of religious experience such as biblical, creedal, and theological expressions.[8] Cousins recognizes that the value of the distinction is that it allows us to concentrate on the often-neglected task of tapping the riches of religious experience before moving too quickly to biblical and doctrinal material. The contemporary need is not so much to demythologize as to help people today discover the power and light of the mystery that surrounds them.

In trying to clarify the transcendental function of mystagogical models it may help to recall some of Ian Ramsey's thoughts on models and disclosure.[9] For him, models point to particular familiar situations which can be used to understand less familiar ones. Religious models also have a "qualifier" which indicates the direction in which we are to push our interpretation of the familiar situation. Thus, the phrase 'First Cause' brings to mind ordinary causal situations but also suggests the need to posit a cause which precedes and unites all causal explanations. In this way we discover the situation for the logical placing of the word 'God'.[10] The function of such religious models is to disclose situations which involve "odd discernment" and "total commitment." He describes these disclosure moments in terms of "coming alive," "the penny dropping," the "ice breaking," and "the light dawning." In other words, one of the tasks of religious models is to facilitate insight into the mysterious character of situations involving structures or patterns of "universal significance." Ramsey's notion of disclosure corresponds closely to the primary function of our mystagogical models, a function which could be summarized as provoking insight into the mystery dimension of human existence.

In examining the disclosure function it is helpful to recall Heidegger's insistence that to disclose means not to infer but "to lay open."[11] An explanatory footnote by the translators, Macquarrie and Robinson, adds:

> To say that something has been 'disclosed' or 'laid open' in Heidegger's sense, does not mean that one has any detailed awareness of the contents which are thus 'disclosed', but rather that they have been 'laid open' to us as implicit in what is given, so that they may be made explicit to our awareness by further analysis or discrimination of the given, rather than by any inference from it.[12]

This is a good reminder that our models are intended, not to give specific knowledge about an object, but rather to light up a dimension which is implicit in experience and which requires further specification.

The function of the models can also be viewed as re-presenting either an aspect of human experience which has been forgotten or "possible modes-of-being-in-the-world that can become actualized by us."[13] Thus the mystagogical models function symbolically, not as mere possibilities or as accomplished actualizations, but as representative of an authentic mode of human existence which stands open to the mystery dimension of experience. In other words, they speak of genuine human possibilities and bring to conscious awareness hidden human potentialities which already involve a relationship to the source and goal of our transcendentality.

Finally, we could say that the function of the mystagogical models is to facilitate the movement of the perception of mystery from the transcendental to the categorical level. They are designed to help people come to a conscious, articulated awareness of the mystery which is always affecting consciousness even if only in a preconceptual, unobjectified, unthematic manner. It is a matter of lighting up the sense of mystery which may be only dimly or vaguely perceived. In addition, the models tend to direct or slant the objectification toward an interpretation of the mystery as gracious, which in turn provides the basis for denominating it as "God." We could think of this as a very limited effort at a categorical mystagogy which relates certain aspects of human experience to particular Christian interpretations, in this case the doctrine of the existence of the holy mystery which we call "God."

We should note here that if the models are internally coherent and faithful to the full range of experience, then these very characteristics also serve as the first step in a validation of their claim to be true. The fact that they have meaning (internal coherence) and are meaningful (thematize significant areas of human experience)[14] gives them an initial validity, especially if we accept the idea that one of the criteria of the truth claims of theological propositions is how far "they bring to light and faithfully testify to the fundamental revelation of man's being-in-the-world."[15] Therefore, we could say that the models not only disclose and thematize mystery, but provide the first step in the validation of their truth claims, a validation which then must be completed by the use of a transcendental method.

2. To accomplish their mystagogical tasks the models must be properly constructed. Ideally, I envision them as consisting of a phenomenology of a particular segment of human existence, elements of a metaphysical-theological anthropology, and more poetic or colorful expressions of the ideas contained in the analysis. Let us look briefly at these three elements in turn.

(a) The phenomenology will attempt to describe human existence in a way that avoids all reductionism and stays open to the whole of human experience. This method (when broadly conceived as careful description which includes analyses of cognitive consciousness, everyday experience, and the symbolic aspects of existence) is well suited for disclosing the mystery dimension of human experience. We can find in various authors examples of this approach: Shubert Ogden's analysis of our basic confidence in life (or "existential faith" as he calls it), which opens up the question of an ultimate creative ground for this fundamental trust;[16] Bernard Lonergan's analysis of being-in-love without restriction, which is experienced as a gift and raises the question of an ultimate source of this gift;[17] Paul Tillich's phenomenology of the various forms of anxiety, which points to an ultimate source (which he calls the "God above God") of the courage to deal with life's meaninglessness;[18] Max Scheler's use of a "phenomenological philosophy" to examine the process of repentance (guilt, conscience, common responsibility, forgiveness, etc.), which if it is not prematurely interpreted will bring before the mind "the mysterious outline of an eternal and infinite Judge."[19]

All of these men make use of descriptive analyses to look at particular aspects of human experience with the purpose of bringing to light a transcendent point of reference which grounds the experience. In our models we will show that our questioning and our freedom necessarily imply the presence of mystery.

(b) The second component of our models can be called the "ontological element" and involves analyses of the universal and necessary structures of human existence expressed in philosophical language. This ontological element is meant to complement the descriptive analysis in three ways: by providing the metaphysical basis for the phenomenology of human activity, by specifying the descriptive language through more precise conceptual language, and by trying to relate both the particular activities (questioning, for example) and the ontological structures to their ultimate ground. Concretely, it is a matter of combining a particular element in the essential structure of human beings with a corresponding phenomenology in order to create a coherent model of a particular aspect of human experience which will reveal a transcendent realm. For example, a description of persons as infinite questioners will be joined to elements of a metaphysics of human knowing in order to indicate the presence of a mystery dimension in all human questioning.

The inclusion of these ontological considerations can be clarified by contrasting it with Langdon Gilkey's method. Making use of a distinction from Heidegger, Gilkey describes his prolegomenon as an ontic analysis which is "a description of the kinds of experiences human beings enjoy in being in the world, rather than an analysis of the ontological structures of either human being or Being generally."[20] While he recognizes that his type of phenomenology implies an ontology, he does not see the value of making it explicit. He is content to describe various aspects of lived experience in order to disclose the dimension of ultimacy. While I agree that some type of ontic analysis or phenomenology should precede metaphysical considerations, especially in dealing with secularized individuals, it seems that there are advantages in including an ontological analysis.

First of all, it renders the insights uncovered by phenomenology more communicable. If a particular interpretation of human experience can be shown to be based on the essentials of human nature, then it can be presented as both universal and necessary. The use of philosophical language provides a precision that descriptive language lacks. A more comprehensive framework can be established which makes the individual analysis more intelligible and enables us to discern general patterns. All of these considerations indicate that communication of the results of a purely descriptive analysis is facilitated by the addition of ontological considerations. Second, it enables us to deal better with the question of truth claims. Once the meaningfulness of a religious interpretation is established, it is natural to wonder if it is true—the kind of question that requires ontological analysis. Even in dealing with those who deny the possibility of any metaphysics, it seems better to challenge them by trying to make explicit the ontological presuppositions involved in any interpretation of existence, rather than to accept implicitly their premise by eschewing all philosophical discussion. Finally, the inclusion of an ontological analysis provides us with a helpful organizing principle. It is possible to relate a great variety of experience to a particular aspect of human existence and ultimately to our essential nature. The examination of ontological structures may suggest a further look at particular types of experience that a simple sociological or psychological survey may have missed. Taken together, these points constitute the rationale for including both phenomenological and ontological elements in our mystagogical models.

We have been speaking about the "ontological element" in order to distinguish it from the phenomenological material and to indicate that it concerns universal and necessary structures or essential characteristics expressed in philosophical language. However, the term needs further clarification. In the actual models we are not dealing directly with a general ontology, that is, with an attempt to uncover the universal and necessary characteristics of being in general. It is rather a matter of making use of material drawn from a metaphysical or theological anthropology. We are interested in the essential structures of the human existent which ground particular areas of self-experience. If we adopt a three-step model of the transcendental method which includes phenomenology, transcendental reduction (uncovering a priori conditions in the subject), and transcendental deduction (deducing the general structures of the object of subjective activity), then we could say that our models concentrate on the first two steps and leave the bulk of the deductive effort till the later discussion of the vindication of their truth claims. In other words, the models contain a reductive analysis which tries to uncover the universal and necessary structures in human existence rather than in being in general. In brief, therefore, our term 'ontological element' refers primarily to a metaphysical anthropology.

(c) The third component of our models can be termed the "poetic or rhapsodic[21] element." This is an attempt to express the insights revealed by the descriptive analysis in vivid, colorful, poetic language which is designed to evoke a responsive chord in the reader. In this regard, we should recall a few points made previously; since mystagogy is more invitation than indoctrination, it should use an evocative language in order to help the listeners to discover the sense of mystery in themselves; poetic or symbolic expressions are better suited for this task than precise conceptual language; mystagogy should risk the use of evocative language even though it is open to the charge of being meaningless or unverifiable.

The discussion of evocative language should include a note on the importance of symbol, image, metaphor, and myth in mediating our self-understanding.[22] Symbolic language is particularly well suited to express the deeper dimensions of our experience which defy a strictly literal rendering. Striking metaphors can jar our usual ways of seeing reality and open up the realm of mystery. Images and myths shape our consciousness and our behavior, often in a prereflective way. It is obvious that an effective mystagogy must be on the lookout for imaginative material which will appeal to the particular audience addressed.

It is important to produce a coherent model in which the phenomenological, ontological, and poetic parts reinforce each other and form an intelligible, consistent whole. Ideally we want a package in which the three factors work together to disclose the mystery dimension in a particular area of human experience. Our intention is reminiscent of a statement of Paul Tillich:

> The test of a phenomenological description is that the picture given by it is convincing, that it can be seen by anyone who is willing to look in the same direction, that the description illuminates other related ideas, and that it makes the reality which these ideas are supposed to reflect understandable.[23]

Although he was speaking of phenomenology only, these criteria could be used to specify the ideal qualities of our models as a whole: convincing, because the descriptions are faithful to the full range of experience and uncover recognizable patterns; involving, because the person addressed is moved to participate in a process of self-discovery; integrating, because individual experiences and their objectification are seen as part of a larger pattern which reflects our essential transcendentality; revealing, because a transcendent dimension is disclosed and thematized as the absolute mystery present in all experience.[24] Thus, we have an ideal picture of how we would like our integrated mystagogical models to function.

III. THE NEED FOR DIVERSE MODELS

Reality is richer than any particular representation of it. Self-experience is so varied that persons can never comprehend themselves from a single viewpoint. It is this fact which dictates the need for a number of models in trying to reveal a transcendent sphere in human experience. Ian Ramsey, in discussing the fact that reality or the cosmos discloses itself with a mysterious richness, says:

> This illustrates, in fact, an important general principle, viz., that to talk about what a cosmic disclosure discloses we shall need a never-ending succession of phrases which can combine in parts to give a never-ending series of metaphorical inroads. In this way theology demands and thrives on a diversity of models; theological discourse must never be uniformly flat. Eccentricity, logical impropriety is its very life blood. The way theological discourse builds up from a subtle selectivity between those various areas of discourse which an endless number of metaphors and models bring with them is not 'death by a thousand qualifications'. Rather it is life by a thousand enrichments.[25]

What Ramsey says of theology in general is surely true for the mystagogical function: many diverse models enrich our understanding of a reality that always remains mysterious.

The need for diversity is also indicated from the viewpoint of those addressed. People obviously differ according to background, temperament, and interests and therefore find themselves more attuned to one type of experience than others. A modern mystagogy must try to determine where contemporary interests and sensibilities are centered, but surely this cannot be pinned down to one area. It is interesting to recall the types of experience favored by some contemporary authors: Gilkey deals with the experience of contingency, relativity, temporality, and freedom;[26] Tillich, standing with many in the existential tradition, stresses the experience of anxiety as opposed to fear;[27] Macquarrie examines the experience of tension between possibility and facticity, rationality and irrationality, responsibility and impotence, anxiety and hope, individual and community;[28] Lonergan analyzes questioning[29] and being in love;[30] Buber puts the emphasis on interpersonal relationships;[31] Tracy examines the world of science, morality, and everyday experience;[32] Ogden looks at man's moral beliefs and his experience of basic confidence;[33] John Dunne analyzes renunciation, death, time, and love;[34] J.G. Davies draws on personal relationships, sexual relations, and work;[35] Peter Berger reflects on play, hope, humor, and the propensity for order;[36] Gabriel Moran examines the relational character of human existence, including experiences described as active-passive, conscious-unconscious, dependent-independent;[37] Schillebeeckx examines fundamental trust[38] as does Hans Küng;[39] Henry Duméry analyzes human freedom.[40] The diversity of the experiences employed by these authors who are interested in reaching people today reinforces the point that modern mystagogy will have to tap a wide variety of experiences in order to be effective in today's world. In other words, the two models I am presenting in the next chapter are only part of a much larger effort that is needed.

CHAPTER SEVEN

Models of Mystery

AS A CONTRIBUTION to the mystagogical task we will develop here two "models of mystery": one based on human questioning, the other on human freedom.

I. THE INFINITE QUESTIONER

1. We human beings are the ones who ask questions. This fact seems indisputable. If someone did deny it, we could point out that he is implicitly affirming the statement by questioning our interpretation. More importantly, our experience is clear on the matter: we want answers, we enjoy discovering, we find a certain satisfaction in learning, we are curious about many things. There seems to be within us a psychological tension which seeks release in learning:

> It is that tension, that drive, that desire to understand, that constitutes the primordial 'Why?' Name it what you please, alertness of mind, intellectual curiosity, the spirit of inquiry, active intelligence, the drive to know. Under any name, it remains the same and is, I trust, very familiar to you.
> This primordial drive, then, is the pure question. It is prior to any insights, any concepts, any words, for insights, concepts, words, have to do with answers; and before we look for answers, we want them; such wanting is the pure question.[1]

Sometimes we find ourselves assailed by doubts and are moved to seek answers. On other occasions we are prompted to question by a certain wonder or amazement in the face of reality. Whatever the precise cause of our spirit of inquiry, we do experience ourselves as never totally satisfied by the particular knowledge we acquire.[2] Each item of new knowledge seems instead to open up larger horizons which in turn expand rather than diminish our questioning. New experiences demand deeper and richer understanding. Our new insights must be validated by more precise judgments. The truth we have attained seeks a place in the wider context of all our acquired knowledge. Our drive to understand moves us from experience to understanding to judgment in a process that continuously generates new questions and has no clear limit. It is true that we also have very opposite experiences: our curiosity is dulled, certitude is in control over doubt, new experiences are limited, the imagination is dormant, new insights lead to dead ends, speculative questions are uninteresting, the framework of our knowledge is relatively stable. And yet our experience tells us that this state of inertia is neither complete nor permanent and that our innate drive to understand has a way of breaking through to consciousness and rekindling the questioning process. Taking our experience as a whole, we can say that we do have an unrestricted desire to know which nothing finite can satisfy. An analysis of the questioning process reveals us as self-transcendent knowers who are open to being in general. In whatever way we go on to specify "being in general," it is clear that our description reveals a dimension to our questioning which is beyond the empirical and finite. Therefore, we could legitimately describe ourselves as infinite questioners whose ultimate objective could be termed "mystery."

Our questioning can also be analyzed from a different angle.[3] Not only do we ask about things and other people but our inquiry also extends to ourselves. Our motives, our relationships, our worldly activities, our deepest secrets are all subject to questioning. But even more importantly, we call ourselves as a whole into question. We want to know: What is my life all about? Where do I fit in the big picture? Is there any final meaning to my existence? What is the true source of my being? Can I confidently resign myself to death? In all these questions we are concerned, not with partial matters, but with our lives as a totality; not with particular questions, but with the general characteristics of reality; not with finite concerns, but with the infinite. Despite, or perhaps because of, its comprehensive character this fundamental question often lies submerged beneath the surface of our consciousness only to emerge as the result of particular experiences. For example, an individual undergoes an ecstatic experience of peace and integration which causes him to ponder the source of this gift; a person in facing his own death suddenly realizes his radical contingency and wonders if he can entrust himself to the mystery that surrounds him; a mother feeling the pressure of caring for her children wonders where she gets the strength to go on; a father secretly

ponders whether his efforts to support his family are really worthwhile; a person immersed in the world of science finds herself asking
if the intelligibility she observes in the world is possible without an
intelligent source; an individual wrestling with a particular moral
problem begins asking why he should be moral at all and thus moves
from the ethical realm to the dimension of transcendence. In all of
these examples the one fundamental question about our existence as
a whole, which so often lies dormant, is brought to awareness. Of
course, this process could be mediated by any particular experience,
and it becomes a matter of self-reflection to see if and how this has
occurred.

To those who do not explicitly recognize the existence or the
meaningfulness of the ultimate question we should point out that
life itself poses this question. It is really not dependent on speculative thought, explicit recognition, or any particular formulation.
Even if it is denied or rejected, it remains true that "each of us is
grazed at least once, perhaps more than once, by the hidden power
of this question, even if he is not aware of what is happening to
him."[4] Perhaps we could even say that life continuously puts the
question to us since it forces us in all our actions to assume, at least
implicitly, a position on the meaningfulness or absurdity of life and
to make choices which reflect our ultimate values. When our existence is viewed in this way, we are constantly faced with the deepest
and most comprehensive question which admits of no simple, clear,
or final answer. The question is so much a part of us and the answer
so elusive that we find a resonance in the statement "Man is the
question for whom there is no answer."[5]

The real problem with the ultimate question is, not its reality or
importance, but the temptation to escape it. Facing this question in
either its explicit or implicit form can produce great anxiety because
it reveals our radical contingency and total dependence.[6] We suddenly realize that we do not control our own existence and are
subject to a power that is beyond us. The great temptation at this
point is to repress the ultimate question and to settle for the com-
fortable world of limited questions and answers. There is an apparent security involved in solving puzzles, finding solutions to technical
problems, and figuring out how to control things, especially in comparison to wrestling with the fundamental question and the incomprehensible mystery it implies. However, we try to escape the great
question at our own peril. To the degree that it recedes from consciousness we forget who we truly are. Our existence becomes flat as
we concentrate exclusively on controlling individual problems. The

deepest sources of our joys and frustrations cannot be examined. We become prey to strange demons that we do not understand. The basis for genuine human relationships begins to fade. It becomes increasingly difficult to focus our energies and to maintain our commitments. We lose sight of what it is all about and where we fit into the larger picture. It seems that if the great question ever disappeared entirely, we would sink into a subhuman existence.

In fact, all attempts to escape the question amount to a neurotic flight from reality and in the long run cannot succeed. Rather than our being haunted by the repressed question, it seems far better to face it directly. This means moving into a realm of mystery where we are forced to admit our contingency, to accept our dependence on a source we do not control, to respond to a summons from beyond our familiar world, to submit to a power greater than ourselves. Objections to such submission can be heard: this kind of talk makes no sense in a scientific age, such a plunge into the unknown is too frightening, it is better not to think or talk about such mysterious matters, more data and certainty are needed before taking this risk, it is not really so mysterious as it first seems. However, others say the question and its demands cannot be forbidden. It is built into our very being. We are persons who combine infinite longings with finite capabilities, and therefore we cannot avoid the question of whether our desires will ultimately reach fulfillment or be doomed to frustration. We awake to find ourselves on a journey not of our own choosing and must wonder where it leads and whether it has a final destination. Our daily activities absorb our attention, but periodically we must ask if it is all worthwhile. In fact, the great fundamental question that we are lurks on the edge of our consciousness. It can be eclipsed for a time, at a price, but it always retains the power to claim our attention and drive us again into the realm of mystery.

2. This descriptive analysis can be supplemented by ontological considerations which attempt to root human questioning in the essential structures of human existence. It is an effort to establish the a priori conditions in persons that make it possible for them to ask the comprehensive question about themselves and being. How must human beings be constituted in order to inquire about the mystery of life? Human questioning and its infinite scope, or mystery dimension, have been revealed by our phenomenological analysis. Now we must determine how this fact can be explained in terms of a metaphysical and theological anthropology. Thus, we are making use of a transcendental method in the sense of trying to uncover the essential

conditions within a knowing subject which make a particular cognitive act possible.

(a) The fact that we *can* call ourselves as a whole into question is intelligible only on condition that we are spirit.[7] Let us now try to explain and demonstrate this thesis which emphasizes the possibility, as opposed to the necessity, of questioning. As we begin to question, we find ourselves already immersed in the world.[8] As physical beings we are united with the rest of the material world. Through our body we are in contact with a whole environment composed of people and things. Through our senses we are outside ourselves and in touch with a larger world. In short, we begin the questioning process as receptive knowers who are immersed in the material world and dependent on it. If we are so tied to the material world, then how can we question it or ourselves? How can we distance ourselves from it in order to ask questions about it? If we begin our questioning as sentient knowers who are united with the objects of our sense knowledge, then the real problem is, not bridging the gap between ourselves and the things known, but explaining how we can distinguish ourselves from this world of known objects in order to become truly human knowers. With this assumption, a metaphysical anthropology then tries to determine what conditions necessarily exist in human beings that allow them to question themselves as a whole despite their immersion in the world.

We can address this problem by examining the process of abstraction involved in human knowing.[9] Human beings are characterized by the fact that they are able to know universal essences which exist in particular things. In fact, objective knowledge is always a reference of a universal idea to a particular reality. But such a reference implies that we as knowers have detached or disengaged the content of the universal from all particulars. This, in turn, implies that we have distanced ourselves from the material world with which we are originally united through sensibility. The fact that we have been able to form universal concepts means that we have been able to turn back to ourselves and place particular realities over against ourselves as objects. This ability to "return to self" is characteristic of spirit as opposed to sense. The more being or greater intensity of being that an entity possesses, the more self-presence or self-luminosity it is able to attain. Since, as was noted, this ability to be self-present is an essential characteristic of spirit, it could be said that the more spiritual a being is, the more complete can be the return to self and the greater the opportunity to achieve self-realization. Now, since we are able to achieve sufficient distance from our world to ask the comprehensive and ultimate question about ourselves, this ability must be attributed to our spiritual nature. Persons can call themselves into question precisely because they are spirit.

The process of abstraction can be analyzed from another viewpoint. Humans can know universals because they are able to perceive the object known by the senses as limited, as not fulfilling all the possibilities of its essential form. The knower realizes that a particular tree does not exhaust the possibilities of "treeness," and in this way he universalizes the concept by detaching it from this particular tree and making it applicable to all trees. This universalizing abstraction is possible only if we in some way apprehend or reach toward the whole range of these possibilities in a dynamic movement which goes beyond every particular object without ever grasping the totality.

In accord with this line of thought it can be said that we are able to question because we are not totally identified with the objects of sense intuition but overflow them in a dynamism that reveals the questionableness of all finite reality, including ourselves. We can ask the comprehensive question because we are already with being as a whole through our transcending apprehension, which reaches out to the totality of all that is without being able to grasp it. If we conceive of spirit in terms of its dynamic openness to the infinite, then we have come back to our original thesis: persons are able to question because they are spirit. We can call ourselves into question not only because we can distance ourselves from the world in a return to self but also because we possess a dynamism characteristic of spirit which is not content with a limited sense intuition or any particular knowledge but which intends an infinite horizon.

The main thesis that the possibility of human questioning is rooted in our spiritual nature can also be demonstrated by examining the process of making judgments.[10] Human beings not only exist as part of an environment but make judgments about it, thereby creating it into an objective world which stands over against themselves. Through our affirmations we shape and order our world, and thus show ourselves to be more than simply passive beings abandoned to a material environment. We are rather subjects able to differentiate ourselves from the objects of our judgment and able to subsist in ourselves.

A closer look at the inner logic of human judgments shows that they do not merely consist in a linking of concepts in the mind but involve the formation of an affirmative synthesis in which a universal concept is referred to a particular reality. It is in this act of referring the universal (which the knower has abstracted in the return to self) to a concrete reality in the world that persons are revealed as subjects over against the world. In other words, judgment is only possible on the condition of the knower's return to self, which is, as we have seen, characteristic of spirit. Now the connection with our ability to question becomes more evident when it is recalled that we not only make particular judgments but also judge about our world as a whole. This judgment is implicitly contained in our response to the comprehensive question of life. Thus, the question about ourselves as a whole is posed by existence itself, and a judgment on it is unavoidably given in the way life is lived. Again, such a judgment is possible only because we have distanced ourselves from all particular realities and returned to ourselves where we confront the ultimate question and respond to it. In short, persons are able to question because they are spirit, and this is revealed in an analysis both of abstraction and of judgment. A phenomenology which discloses the dimension of mystery in human questioning is rooted in an anthropology which views persons as spirit, both in their ability to return to self and in their dynamic openness to the infinite.

(b) Human beings *necessarily* pose the ultimate and comprehensive question, and this is intelligible only on condition that they are finite spirits immersed in the material world. In this thesis we are beginning, not simply with the fact of questioning (as we did in the first thesis on the possibility of questioning), but with a claim that this questioning is necessary. The necessity arises out of existence itself and is present whether it is recognized or not and whether it is accepted or denied. It is true that we can avoid any particular question, but we cannot escape from the ultimate question which is implied in all our human activity. For in all knowing and willing we necessarily, if implicitly, are present to ourselves and take a stand toward ourselves. Even if the fundamental questions do not rise to explicit consciousness, life itself poses the question of meaning or absurdity, and people answer it implicitly by their daily choices. Pursuing this point further would bring us to the problem of freedom, but here it is enough to establish that human beings necessarily call themselves as a whole into question. We are still faced with the problem of determining what it is about humans that accounts for this fact. What are the transcendental a priori conditions which make questioning necessary? How are persons constructed so that they necessarily call themselves into question? Answering this is made more difficult when we recall our previous discussion of human beings as spirit. Since persons are dynamic openness and unlimited transcendence, it might be assumed that they are totally self-present and therefore in no need of questioning. However, since questioning does occur, we must look for an explanation of the knower's limitations. In other words, because we first established persons as spirit, we must now inquire after the conditions in knowers that prevent them from achieving total self-possession and which make continual questioning necessary.

We can attack this problem from a number of angles. First, we should recall our starting point. Persons begin to question as individuals immersed in the material world and given over to the other through their senses. The essential openness of human beings to the infinite was established as a condition for the possibility of their knowing. This unlimited openness does not vitiate the starting point, which remains our immersion in the concrete here and now of the material world. As a matter of fact, human beings possess a virtual (as opposed to actual) transcendence to the infinite. We reach out to the infinite, but without ever catching up with our anticipation. The fact that we continue to question shows that we know something of ourselves, but not everything; that we return to self, but never achieve total self-possession; that we are both present and absent to ourselves.[11] We are limited creatures who can actualize ourselves only successively and gradually. We cannot comprehend the whole of being all at once, because if we did there would be no explanation for our continued questioning. Persons are spirit, but not absolute spirit. Since we necessarily continue to question and always remain a question to ourselves, we must be a limited or finite spirit. Mystery is not swallowed up in total comprehension but is an abiding dimension of human existence.

Our limitation as transcendent knowers can also be shown by looking again at the process of abstraction. We begin our questioning as individuals present to particular finite objects through our senses. From this involvement in sense data the human knower is able to attain a universal concept and apply it to a particular concrete reality in a process that involves a return to self. This ability to universalize is based on our spiritual dynamism which transcends every finite reality. However, this dynamism is never perceived simply and purely in itself but is always known only in the experience of limitation. In other words, the fact that no finite reality exhausts the knower's transcending anticipation or fills up the horizon of the spiritual drive not only enables the process of abstraction but reveals the finitude and limitation of the knower. No particular knowledge is totally satisfying. Actual human knowledge never catches up with the full range of possibilities. No particular object can fill the infinite scope of our dynamic openness. The spirit's drive for total self-possession and a complete grasp of being itself cannot be achieved in human beings. Persons remain infinite questioners immersed in mystery because they are limited finite spirit.

Now to deepen our analysis we must seek the condition of possibility for persons to be finite spirit. What accounts for the limitations found in human knowing? What are the a priori conditions which ground our continued questioning?[12] We must go back to our starting point. Persons begin their knowing by contacting the world outside themselves through their senses. Since a pure spirit is always self-present, there must be a nonspiritual principle in human beings which accounts for their being outside of themselves and immersed in the world. This principle can be called "materiality."[13]

The same point can be established in another way. Since we call ourselves into question, it follows that we know something about ourselves, which makes the question possible, but not everything, which makes it necessary. But a pure spirit is always totally self-present and completely aware of itself. Therefore humans are not pure spirit but possess a limiting, nonspiritual principle.

The argumentation can be repeated from a slightly different perspective. Persons are receptive knowers since their self-awareness is not innate but derives from their involvement in the world. This means that we are not pure spirit despite our unlimited transcendentality, because the nature of spirit is to determine itself. Since human knowers are affected by the material world, we must posit a principle in them which makes this possible. We arrive again at a nonspiritual principle, or, as we have called it, "materiality."

We had to follow this line of argumentation because, having first established our spiritual nature which implies infinite openness, we had to account for the actual limitations we experience. In the process we have demonstrated the necessity of positing a material principle in human beings. It is a case, not of simply observing that we have a body, but of establishing that the finite spirit must be characterized by materiality. From this perspective we can say that the human spirit necessarily embodies itself and that the human intellect must posit sensibility as its mode of knowing. In addition, our materiality means that human existence does not just happen to be carried out in a space-time framework but that we are necessarily immersed in a world of space and time.

In summary, we have seen that materiality is the limiting principle in human knowing and the a priori condition for the fact that human beings must question. We continually call ourselves into question because, as material beings united with the world through our senses, we can never achieve a final total self-possession but can only gradually realize ourselves in space and time. A phenomenology which reveals a mystery dimension to human questioning is based on an anthropology which views persons as finite spirit immersed in a material world.

(c) For the purpose of analysis we have examined separately the possibility of questioning based on spirit and the necessity of questioning rooted in materiality. Of course, individuals carry out their questioning as single subjects whose cognitive acts are a unified whole. Thus we are always: known to ourselves, but in process of learning about ourselves; present to being as a whole, but never grasping it completely; involved in a process of going out to the world and returning to self; abstracting and turning to the sensible world in a single knowing process; self-present, but never totally so; reaching for the infinite, but never grasping it. It is the fundamental dialectic between these elements in the one human existent that makes questioning both possible and necessary. Persons can and must call themselves into question because they are the finite, material, sensible spirit immersed in a world of space and time. We remain a mystery to ourselves because we are spirit in the world sustained and drawn by the absolute mystery.

II. HUMAN FREEDOM

1. For a number of reasons it is difficult to work out a phenomenology of human freedom. First of all, it does not appear as one particular aspect of our experience nor as an objective phenomenon which can directly be discovered in our consciousness; therefore it can be easily overlooked or denied. Introspection fails to uncover a specific area of freedom which is clearly delineated from regions of determined behavior. In addition, the topic of freedom seems so comprehensive that it is difficult to break it down in order to analyze it. In the contemporary world the word 'freedom' has come to sum up all our hopes and desires and to stand for the whole of human existence. Thus Sartre says that freedom "is not a quality added on or a *property* of my nature. It is very exactly the stuff of my being."[14] If we do try to break down the topic, we end up with a great variety of major themes: the nature of freedom, freedom vs. determinism, the individual in community, societal constraints, free-

dom and time, death as the finality of freedom, freedom and responsibility, and so on. Even this partial list suggests the difficulty of discussing freedom in any kind of comprehensive or systematic way. A final problem to be noted is the claim that the very talk of freedom is harmful because it falsifies human experience and prevents us from properly organizing useful control systems to program human behavior.[15]

Despite these problems let us stay open to the following descriptive analysis of freedom to see if it strikes a responsive chord.[16]

(a) We experience ourselves in many ways as the product of forces over which we have no control. We did not choose our parents, nationality, historical period, or sex; our physical makeup and intellectual capacity are received; death can overpower us against our will. In addition, when we begin to examine our particular actions, it is possible to uncover hidden motivations and sociological pressures which seem to shift responsibility away from ourselves. Today the empirical human sciences facilitate this escape by bringing to light various causes or forces outside our conscious control which program our behavior. For example, depth psychology reveals to us the immense power and influence of the unconscious. Furthermore, the sciences have the tendency to take a particular causal connection and to elevate it into a total explanation of human existence which ends up denying human freedom.[17] And so from many angles our self-experience today includes large amounts of determinism and necessity. In fact, it becomes doubtful if we can point to any particular decision of ours and unequivocally state that it is the product of freedom and not determined by other causes.

If we grant this much to the determinists, are we not in danger of destroying freedom and thus dissolving the dimension of mystery implied in free activity? In response let us reflect on this paradoxical claim: "Man experiences himself precisely as subject and person insofar as he becomes conscious of himself as the product of what is radically foreign to him."[18] We could paraphrase this statement by saying that we experience our freedom precisely in the midst of necessity and determinism. This implies that we are able to step back and analyze the causes of our behavior and thereby achieve consciousness of ourselves as the product of various factors. In doing this we affirm ourselves as greater than the sum total of the causal factors. In calling ourselves and our behavior into question we experience ourselves as transcending every particular factor in our makeup. Thus we are revealed as personal subjects who must take up an attitude toward our existence as a whole. In other words, we are consigned to ourselves or placed in our own hands. This is true even if we try to shift all responsibility away from ourselves, for in doing so we know ourselves as conscious subjects who are acting knowingly and willingly. Hence, even in denying our freedom we are acting as free individuals. In summary, we know ourselves as the ones who are given over to ourselves, and in this we know that we are freely responsible for our lives as a whole even if we remain doubtful whether our individual actions are determined or not.

It is important to note explicitly the direction taken by this descriptive analysis. It is an attempt to ground freedom in a realm that is beyond the reach of empirical science. It is prepared to admit and even encourage the effort of science to explore human behavior in terms of identifiable causal factors. We are trying, not to establish a tiny area of freedom in the midst of massive necessity and determinism, but rather to locate freedom at a deeper level where we transcend the component parts of our existence and have an ultimate responsibility for ourselves as a whole.

We could say that it is an effort to establish "transcendental freedom" while avoiding a direct defense of "categorical freedom." Now this transcendental freedom cannot be understood on the model of a computer, which is a self-directing but enclosed system. Rather, our ability to confront ourselves with all our future possibilities indicates an open system which is not subject to empirical verification and which indicates a transcending dimension that could well be termed "mystery." This means that mystery appears very early in the analysis, not as a particular circumscribed region next to areas of explainable behavior, but as a dimension of our free disposal of ourselves as a whole. The claim is that we can become aware of this mystery when we reflect on our transcendental freedom.

Once our free subjectivity is established, we can further specify our freedom by saying that it is the power to determine ourselves in a final and definitive way.[19] Certain experiences point to this characteristic. We might recall times when we have made serious decisions and sensed that we would never be the same afterward. Perhaps the choice was so deeply rooted and touched so much of our lives that we knew we could never go back on it and that it would always continue to influence our future. Are there also times when we realize that many small decisions are shaping our personality and that we are taking on permanent character traits based on these choices? Is there a way in which we know that a self is being created which has a permanency that outlasts each particular act of our freedom? And what of our longings? Do we not desire a permanent validity for our lives, a final meaning to all our struggles, a lasting significance for the self we have created? Finally, have we known moments when we wanted to find a way to give complete expression to our personalities, to sum up what we stand for and value through a particular decisive act?

If we can recall experiences like this, then we are in a position to understand the claim that freedom is, not simply a matter of choosing this or that, but the capacity to determine oneself once and for all. Through our individual decisions we make ourselves to be what we will be forever. Our self is not like a stage on which our individual actions play out their bit parts, only to depart, leaving the stage unchanged. Rather, the self resembles a storehouse in which is gathered the true and abiding significance of all our human activity.[20] In this light our freedom is, not simply the ability to change and revise continuously, but the capacity for the infinite and eternal. Our individual actions may fade from memory, and we may esteem them as unconnected and transitory. However, the truth is that in the secret recesses of our being they are combining to shape our character and determine our eternal destiny.[21] Thus we have the power to shape the whole of our existence, to decide for or against ourselves, to achieve or thwart a definitive self-fulfillment, to attain salvation or damnation.

This characteristic of freedom is most clearly manifested in death, where we are called upon to make a final irreversible decision about our life as a whole. This presupposes that we understand death not merely as a passive separation of body and soul but as our freest moment in which we actively sum up our lives.[22] Actually, death is the only chance we have to achieve our definitive self-fulfillment, since on this earth our fundamental decisions are always open to change and our freedom never integrates all aspects of our personality. Put negatively, if we had to continue in this life forever, it would amount to being damned, since the possibility of an eternal, positive validity for all our actions would be eliminated.

Viewing human freedom as the capacity for a definitive self-actualization again reveals a dimension of mystery. We experience this freedom as a gift from a source beyond us and as moving toward a goal that remains fundamentally unknown and unknowable. The power to determine ourselves forever is not really subject to empirical analysis, nor is it open to the direct gaze of introspection. It is not a particular power which can be analyzed in terms of a larger coordinate system into which it fits. In fact, we cannot attain certitude about whether we are saying yes or no to ourselves in our freedom. We go to death in darkness, not knowing with absolute certainty whether the final free disposal of ourselves is into the absurdity of nothingness or into the hands of a gracious mystery. All of this indicates that the fundamental ability to determine ourselves forever cannot be confined to the realm of the empirically verifiable or rationally intelligible but spills over into a transcendent dimension which can be aptly called "mystery."

In continuing to specify transcendental freedom we can say that it is the power to accept or reject the source and goal of that very freedom.[23] We often experience ourselves as free in relation to particular objects in the sense of not feeling a compulsion to choose this rather than that. No particular good seems to satisfy our desires. It could be argued that such experiences are indications of the existence of an absolute good which functions as the horizon for our free acts. We know individual objects as partial goods only in relation to the good itself, and the insatiable character of our desires points to an infinite goal or absolute good which would quiet the heart. Without developing the argument, it can be said that an analysis of freedom at least suggests a relationship to an absolute good which functions as a transcendent goal.

Now in taking up an attitude toward ourselves we necessarily adopt a position toward this goal of our freedom. More specifically, in achieving our own free self-disposal we are implicitly accepting or rejecting the basis and the term of this capacity. This relationship is present whether we recognize it or not and whether we correctly interpret it or not, since in constructing our own permanent being through our free acts we remain unavoidably dependent on the very source of that power.

In a radical sense our freedom is constituted by the ability to contradict itself. It includes the power to reject the condition of its possibility, even though in the very act of denial the condition is again implicitly affirmed. Put in personal terms, our freedom involves the possibility of saying no to God, which involves the contradiction of denying him while implicitly affirming him as the necessary horizon of the act of rejection. We should note that this analysis does not imply that human beings are in a position of neutrality in relation to the horizon or that a denial is as natural as an affirmation. The point here is simply that human freedom does include the possibility of a culpable and contradictory denial of its very source, even though it is necessarily present as the ground and horizon of all free acts.

In looking for experiential confirmation of this deductive

analysis of freedom toward its ground, we might turn to the times
when we felt in harmony with the universe, at one with the powers
beyond us, integrated within ourselves, at peace with our world,
carried along by a force beyond us, a significant part of a larger
plan. We could take these experiences as indicating that our self-
acceptance involved a proper and life-giving affirmation of the
ground that supports and sustains us. On the negative side we could
recall the stirrings of conscience which trouble, disturb, judge, or
condemn us. At those times we sense that our freedom has led us
astray, put us into self-contradiction, disrupted the proper order of
things, violated some ultimate harmony of things. Again we could
interpret these experiences as indicating not only an alienation from
self but from the ultimate source and goal as well. This whole analysis opens up the dimension of mystery again, since the source and
goal can be understood, not as finite elements within a closed system
of causal connections, but only as transcendent conditions which
make any exercise of freedom possible.

Let us summarize our results so far. In the descriptive analysis
of transcendental freedom we made use of experiences which suggest in turn that we are free subjects, responsible for ourselves as a
whole, able to actualize ourselves in a definitive way, and necessarily
related to the absolute mystery which supports and draws our freedom. By proceeding in this way freedom is revealed, not as a narrow
slice of experience subject to the continued attacks of empirical science, but as a transcendent dimension of human existence as a
whole, which in itself can properly be termed "mystery" since it
cannot be analyzed in terms of a larger system into which it can
logically be placed.

(b) Since transcendental freedom does not exist in some pure
ideal state but is always embodied in particular concrete acts, we
must now examine the ways in which we actually experience the
limitations of freedom. As was noted, our experience tells us that we
do not completely control our existence, that the ability to dispose of
ourselves freely comes from a source outside of ourselves. Furthermore, we make our individual decisions as persons who are already
immersed in an historical situation not of our own choosing. We find
ourselves restricted by various factors: by political, economic, and
social forces; by our heredity, temperament, and past decisions; by
the dominant images, roles, and expectations of our culture; by our
work, suffering, and death. Actually we never escape completely
from the necessities imposed on us, but we are always forced to take
up an attitude toward them. Our personal subjectivity is achieved,

not by completely mastering our historical situation or by escaping from it, but by adopting a particular stance toward it.

Limitations appear again when we consider freedom as self-disposal. Though we want to achieve a total integration and to sum up our life in a luminous free act, we are not able to do so. We find ourselves overwhelmed by the knowledge explosion and by the great variety of choices that are presented to us. We cannot find a comprehensive viewpoint for mastering all available information, nor do we ever actualize all our possibilities for growth and development. Our freedom cannot bring all aspects of our personality under control. We experience ourselves as split, in tension, unable to harmonize the opposing aspects of our existence. In short, our desire for total self-actualization is continuously thwarted because our freedom cannot master all the factors presented to it.

Our longings for a final, definitive self-disposal are also continually frustrated. We experience ourselves as open to change and revision because particular decisions never embrace the totality of our existence but only make room for further decisions. Our general orientation in life seems clear, and then a new experience comes along which challenges our whole direction. Many of our decisions seem to involve only a partial commitment and fail to grasp us in the depths of our being. Much of our life is lived out in routine and habit. Even the deeper decisions involving a serious commitment fail to mobilize all aspects of our being and leave elements warring against our fundamental option. If it is possible to gather ourselves completely and to commit ourselves totally, then it can only occur in death, which remains darkly mysterious to us.

The finite character of our freedom also appears in the analysis of our freely chosen stance vis-à-vis the ground and horizon of our freedom. For we can never be absolutely certain if we have truly accepted this mystery which grounds our freedom, since we have no way to step back and examine it in a larger framework, and we cannot directly apprehend it through introspection. Not only does our fundamental option remain partially veiled but it is subject to temptation. We can never be certain that we will not reverse an existing positive orientation and reject the true goal of our freedom. A no to the horizon of our transcendental freedom always remains possible. Again, freedom as we actually experience it is limited and always coexists with elements of necessity.

Transcendental freedom is always mediated through particular decisions which share in all the limitations and ambiguity of the material finite world. We experience ourselves as situated between the finite and the infinite, and we become aware of this precisely in our ability to transcend all the necessities of existence by freely taking up a position toward them. This extends to the very gift of freedom itself which we did not choose and which we cannot escape, but which we are called upon to accept with a sense of responsibility. Therefore, we can see that finite freedom as we actually experience it points to the dimension of mystery as a condition of its possibility. We sense that our freedom is not our own creation but comes from a transcending source, and we become aware of the limited character of our freedom only because we strive past every finite good in an effort to achieve a final and definitive disposal of ourselves which includes an acceptance of the absolute mystery that grounds the whole process. In summary, we encounter mystery precisely as the ones who cannot escape from limitation and necessity, who are unable to synthesize all the various aspects of our experience and personality, who cannot achieve a total giving of ourselves, and who can never rest secure in the absolute certitude of salvation.

(c) Let us look now at our experience of self-acceptance as a good example of the way our finite freedom is manifested. Consider the overwhelming array of factors beyond our control which we are called upon to accept: our birth into existence; our physical and psychic makeup; our historical and cultural situation; our subjection to the rhythm of time with its growth and decline; our inescapable and burdensome responsibility for ourselves and our world; our unknown and unknowable future; our limited intellectual and emotional capacity; our infinite longings which are never fulfilled in this world; our sufferings both physical and mental; our radical contingency and dependence; our immersion in an ambiguous world with its oppressive institutions and structures; our need for others to share our love; our past decisions, especially the bad ones; our unavoidable death. When we reflect on these factors, we begin to realize how difficult total self-acceptance is and how far we have to go in achieving it. To accept ourselves totally and freely is indeed an always incomplete lifetime task.

It is the great anxiety involved in accepting ourselves in all of our radical contingency that intensifies the problem. Perhaps we experience this most acutely today in having to accept the heavy burden of responsibility for ourselves and our world.[24] Even though we are able to control so much more of our lives these days, it seems that anxiety continues to plague us. The greater our power to plan and shape our future, the more we feel the burden of responsibility and are frightened by the essentially unknowable character of the future. Thus we come to appreciate in a concrete way the general notion that we are condemned to freedom.[25] As we gain greater ability to determine ourselves and to shape our world, we become, not more secure, but, paradoxically, more aware of our finitude, subject to greater anxiety, and more cognizant of the burden of our freedom and responsibility. In this situation the great temptation is to escape from facing the burden of our freedom, to sink into a paralyzed state before our great responsibilities,[26] to avoid a whole-hearted commitment to any particular course of action.[27]

However, try as we might to escape, we cannot avoid the burden of freely taking up a position toward our actual existence. Life itself forces us to at least one fundamental decision about ourselves: whether we accept our existence as meaningful or not. This task may seem odious and the temptation to escape it powerful, but we are summoned to accept this ultimate freedom with courage.

This implies that we are free to accept what is necessarily part of ourselves, to ratify our finiteness. Genuine freedom is rooted in the capacity to accept our essential contingency. Our challenge is to say yes to ourselves, to affirm our lives as we find them, and not to waste our freedom in a useless protest against our fate or to abdicate our freedom in an escape from reality. We may come to understand this better as we contemplate concrete steps for achieving this acceptance. It is helpful to cultivate a rigorous honesty with ourselves that puts us in touch with our deepest negative feelings, especially fears, and unmasks all our attempts at unfounded self-sufficiency. We should strive for a patience with ourselves that puts us at ease with the limits and pace of our growth and maturation. While planning for the future is important, it must be placed in a larger context of accepting an essentially unknowable future which is beyond our control. We must also acquire the facility of calmly passing up many viable opportunities for self-actualization while choosing one particular course of action. We will be able to do this and avoid frustration only if we realize that our self-fulfillment is attained, not by piecing together all possible experiences, but by achieving a proper self-acceptance. Finally, it is vital to overcome the escapist tendencies in our death-denying culture and to work at the business of facing up to our own death. Since death represents limitations and contingency in a radical way, coming to terms with this dark force is crucial in achieving an authentic self-acceptance.

Behind all these approaches it is the acceptance of a gracious mystery encompassing our lives which enables us to accept our finite contingent existence. Our longings in this regard are clear: that the source of our life is gracious, that the unknowable future is benign, that there is wholeness for our scattered and fragmented existence, that there is fulfillment for our deepest desires, that there is fullness of life after death. We sense that if all of this were true, then greater self-acceptance would be possible since we could confidently entrust our contingency to such a gracious mystery.

Are there any indications in our experience that such a trusting attitude is justified? Can we recall times when we have honestly accepted one of our particular limitations and found this to be liberating, when we faced a fear and discovered it was less powerful than we thought, when we fought anxiety by silent meditation and felt an inner peace, when we faced death and found a surprising inner strength? Could we not interpret these experiences as indications that a greater self-acceptance is possible because we are already accepted by the loving mystery that surrounds us?

It is important to realize that there may be an anonymous character to this whole process. The perception of the gracious nature of reality may be vague; it may even be denied or devoid of any explicit articulation including religious objectifications. Self-acceptance may seem to be achieved without any reference to mystery or its benign character. And yet it can be argued that any genuine acceptance of self does at least implicitly involve a belief that the process of life can be trusted. In fact, there must be some sort of positive awareness which makes the self-acceptance possible in the first place.

Consider some of our more successful efforts: moments of sober realism when we have admitted our sinfulness; times when we have exercised a remarkable patience in accepting changes which we could not control; the occasions when we calmly passed up something we wanted to do and still enjoyed the thing we did choose.

Does not this ability to say yes to ourselves in our ambiguity and limitation appear as an unearned and undeserved gift? Does not the power to accept the harsh negative experience of life seem to come from outside ourselves? Does not such self-acceptance already imply a larger framework of meaning that makes it possible? It does seem that if we can recognize and name this source and judge it friendly, the process of self-acceptance is facilitated. However, even without this explicit awareness it remains true that any progress in accepting ourselves is dependent on at least an implicit sense of the graciousness of life. To accept ourselves in all our ambiguity and to do so calmly with faith and hope is already to accept the friendly character of the mystery which surrounds and supports us.

From this viewpoint self-acceptance is the main problem of life. In struggling to achieve it we know the great burden of freedom, the anxiety of facing our limitations and ultimate contingency, the responsibility of shaping our existence. Within this whole process we can discover the dimension of mystery. It is present as the source of our contingent existence, as the ground of the inescapable obligation to take hold of our lives, as the goal of our self-development, as the strength in dealing with our anxiety, as the meaning of the whole effort to achieve self-acceptance.

(d) Besides self-acceptance, finite freedom also realizes itself in human love. As with freedom in general, it is difficult to reflect on love because of its comprehensive and transcendental character. It can properly be understood only from within the experience and not through objective examination. Our attempts to analyze it can only be seen as an effort to disclose a primordial experience that is always richer than any description of it.

Love has to do with reaching out to another person. In genuine love we go out of ourselves and achieve a relationship with a human partner. This can be contrasted with the process of knowing in which we are in contact with others and then possess them intentionally in the return to self. Knowledge is self-presence; love, on the contrary, involves a process in which a person who has achieved a degree of self-possession freely moves toward another unique individual. In love we strive to embrace the other in order that the loved one may be enriched. We move out of the prison of self in an effort to care for another human being. While knowledge occurs in an interior modification of the self, love involves an enactment of self in the other.

Only love can free us from ourselves and bring us a fullness of life. If we are to avoid hating ourselves and being swallowed up in our own emptiness, we must allow ourselves to be drawn out by a love that wills the good of another. This demands a detachment from our own interests and a triumph over our fear of losing our autonomy. To achieve this we must have a point outside of ourselves, a human partner who moves us to transcend ourselves. When we are able to love another unselfishly, we experience a life-giving liberation from the imprisonment of our own egotism.

If we are to love in this genuine way, then we must learn to respect the unique personalities of other people. True love fosters the individuality of others and enables them to become their best selves, to develop their talents, to be true to their own consciences, to become mature persons.[28] We must overcome the temptation to manipulate others by forcing them to conform to an ideal of our own creation. This really amounts to a type of narcissism and betrays the ideal of a liberating and individuating love.

Our description of the ideal lover who reaches out to the beloved leads us into the realm of mystery. The ability to let go of ourselves trustfully implies a confidence in a gracious power greater than our own. A genuine respect for other persons in their uniqueness suggests the existence of an absolute good which grounds their dignity and worth. The dynamism which propels us out of ourselves toward the other implies a power that is beyond our control. In genuine love a dimension of existence is opened up which eludes empirical analysis and can be properly called "mystery."

Not only is love a reaching out and an acceptance of the other, but it is the self-actualization of the lover. Paradoxically, letting go of ourself in giving to the other is the only way of really finding ourself. We can only achieve our true nature through love. Genuine love allows us to forget ourselves, enabling us to live spontaneously in the present; to feel forgiven for sins of the past, freeing us to live wholeheartedly in the now; to imagine a better future, inspiring us to seize current opportunities.

In our ecstatic moments we feel that our love is unique and has never happened before.[29] We feel alive in a new and different way because love liberates in us the very things that constitute our individuality. As we reach out in loving service to others, we discover ourselves in a new way and become aware of the special contributions only we can make. In this experience we know ourselves as persons of unique value. Through a loving commitment to another human being we are forgetful enough of our selfish desires and open enough to reality outside ourselves to be in a position to achieve growth and greater maturity.

Therefore, it can be said that self-fulfillment and willing the good of the other are not mutually exclusive but imply one another since it is only by going out of ourselves toward others that we fully engage ourselves and actualize our potential. We find our happiness precisely in loving other persons. There is no genuine love which is so disinterested and involved with the other that all personal fulfillment is excluded.

When we try to deepen our reflection on self-actualization through love, we are brought back to the perception that the resources for our fulfillment and happiness are not our own property but are found outside of ourselves (and even outside of those we love) in a source which is clearly beyond our control and which we therefore name the "absolute mystery."

Genuine love involves a relationship between persons characterized by mutuality.[30] Simply put, this demands a giving and receiving in which each partner makes a contribution to the relationship and in turn finds support and strength in this interchange. Mutuality is the opposite of a domineering, controlling, one-way relationship. It is, however, predicated, not on an exact equality between the partners, but on each being able to contribute out of their unique individuality. What is needed is a mutual trust based on a fidelity to each other which allows each one to give and receive with confidence. This is vital because of the great risk involved in love. In committing ourselves to others we put our happiness in their hands, give them power to hurt us, and join our future with theirs. Perhaps the great fear is that in opening ourselves completely to another human being, we will lose our autonomy and get swallowed up in the relationship. Only mutual love can overcome this anxiety because it sets up a trusting situation where individuality is fostered and differences are celebrated.

Mutuality implies that love is given without measure. One can never say "I have loved enough" because love is not a law that can be kept but a call to respond ever more generously. It is genuine only if it is always ready to surpass itself. Within such a relationship of mutual love, individuality can be achieved without it devolving into a self-sufficient egoism. The lover must help others to develop their unique personalities by giving them confidence that it is all right to follow out their own best insights.

When we explore the notion of love as a mutual exchange, we again move into the realm of mystery: in fact, this may be one of the best indications of a transcendent dimension in human life. In the experience of love we feel drawn out of ourselves by a force that surprises us by its power. In risking our own happiness by placing ourselves in the hands of another, we act in a mad and improbable way which on rational analysis does not seem to pay off. When we are able to respect and foster the individuality of our loved ones, we are often amazed at the mysterious depths and unsuspected richness that they possess. In our best moments we know that the beloved is not a problem to be solved but a mystery to be treasured.[31] In addition, we desire permanency for our mutual relationships. The language of love is not "for awhile" but "forever." We experience our genuine love as pointing beyond itself in a hope for a lasting meaning. In affirming the value and dignity of our loved ones, we recognize a hope for immortality that goes beyond all empirical evidence. In short, our discussion of mutual love reveals aspects of experience which are clearly not subject to scientific analysis or rational calculation but which call for the language of transcendence and mystery.

So far we have spoken of human love in ideal terms. If the descriptive analysis we have presented strikes responsive chords, it is because we recognize it in our ideals, longings, and hopes as opposed to the concrete ways we actually experience ourselves as lovers. Thus, our best instincts are to abandon the prison of our own emptiness in order to reach out to the other in love, but we often find ourselves caught up in our own selfishness. Our better self knows that we should treasure the other's uniqueness, and yet we fall into patterns of domination or jealousy. We somehow realize that total commitment is liberating, but we shrink from it in an effort to hang on to our autonomy. The ideal of completely open communication is attractive, but our fears hold us back. We dream of a perfect love and an ideal respondent, but all of our experiences fall short. Our desire is to preserve the ecstatic moments and for our relationships to be permanent, and yet time and death take their toll. We would like to be better lovers, but our own sins and limitations get in the way. However, even this contrast (which brings so much disappointment) between the ideal and our actual experience of love raises again the question of mystery. Are our longings doomed to frustration, or is there a final fulfillment for them? Is our sense of the unique value of other persons misguided, or is it founded on the presence of an absolute good? Is our effort to be a better lover foolish, or does it make sense in the final analysis? Is our insatiable desire to love perfectly based on a quirk of fate, or does it flow from a gracious source? Is our search for the ideal lover an absurd venture that must fail, or will it succeed and justify itself as meaningful? To raise such questions, as our existence must, already puts us beyond rational calculation and into a transcendent realm. At the very least, mystery is present as a question posed by our actual experience of love. Are we indeed a "useless passion," or will our love find fulfillment in a gracious mystery which grounds and draws the longings of the heart?

It seems reasonable to offer a positive response to these questions and to suggest that there are clues in our experience of love which point to an absolute and gracious mystery. Have we ever felt in our heart that our love for another has an intrinsic value and abiding worth? Are there times when we managed to love someone even though there was no obvious payoff for us? Have we known times when the needs of our neighbor made absolute and unavoidable claims upon us? Have we felt impulses to reach out lovingly to another even when our normal inclination was to withdraw into ourselves? Have we known the liberating joy of suddenly breaking out of our selfishness and allowing ourselves to surrender to another in love? Have we found that loving others reveals surprising depths and unexpected goodness in them? It seems that in these experiences we have intimations of the existence of a gracious mystery which is the transcendent source of the power of love. Of course, we only come to realize this from within a genuine experience of love which enables us to break out of the prison of selfishness, to reach out to another, to respect and foster their individuality, and to achieve a mutual sharing.

From within the experience of love it is clear that the language of the computer must give way to the language of mystery that points to and evokes the deeper and more significant dimensions of our experience.

2. Now that we have presented a phenomenology of freedom which discloses mystery, we should reinforce our conclusions by grounding them in the ontological structures of human existence. This involves first of all trying to establish freedom as a necessary factor in human life and then determining the essential characteristics of human beings which make this exercise of freedom possible.

In trying to find a solid foundation for human freedom, let us begin by going back to the indisputable fact of human questioning, especially that we call ourselves as a whole into question (or, equivalently, ask the ultimate question about being in general).[32] The fact that we must ask about being itself shows that we do not possess or comprehend it completely and that, therefore, we are finite. Human beings do not cause or control their own existence but receive it from a source outside themselves; otherwise they would not have to question. Hence, we are called upon to take up a stance in relation to our radical contingency, to accept freely the unavoidable fact that we are not the cause of our own being. Since we cannot avoid assuming some attitude toward our dependent situation (even if it is not made explicit), it can be said that we have a necessary relationship to our contingent existence. It is precisely here that the question of freedom first arises since only a free decision can account for the affirmation of something which does not call for this in itself. But human existence, since it is contingent, does not provide sufficient reason from within itself for affirming it necessarily and absolutely. Therefore, if it is to be necessarily posited, such an affirmation must proceed from the free decision of individuals.

In the light of this analysis it is clear that our openness to being in general does not involve knowledge alone but is also a matter of will and freedom. Human questioning, which at first appears simply as a cognitive activity, necessarily includes volitional elements both because questioning implies a desire or striving to know and because it (at least as the ultimate question about being) implies a free decision that human existence and its ground are worth investigating. Therefore, our conclusion is that freedom must be posited as a transcendental condition for the fact that human beings ask the ultimate question. Persons are free spirits whose very openness to the infinite (as revealed by unlimited questioning) can only be fully understood in terms of striving, desire, attitude, and choice—all volitional elements. Human freedom is not established by arguing that particular acts are free rather than determined, but it is posited as the necessary condition for the fact that we call ourselves into question and thereby assume an attitude toward ourselves and the source of our contingent existence. Hence, transcendental freedom is not only a phenomenon revealed by careful description but a metaphysically necessary component of human existence.[33]

Once transcendental freedom is established, we are in a position to discuss freedom of choice, since it is our relationship to the absolute that forms the basis for our ability to choose among various objects. The human spirit manifests its dynamism not only in overflowing every particular item of knowledge in a transcending anticipation of absolute truth but also in surpassing all particular goods in a loving movement toward the absolute good. Within the horizon of this absolute good (which functions as the goal of human transcendence) every particular good is seen as limited and therefore can be chosen or rejected. It is essential for freedom that the absolute good remain incomprehensible, since this insures an open space which can never be filled by an individual object and thus leaves room for choosing among various partial goods. In short, human beings are free to choose because no finite good can totally capture the dynamism of their infinite longing for the good in itself.

An understanding of transcendental freedom also sets the scene for a discussion of human love. Let us begin by exploring Rahner's statement "The only ultimate structure of the person which adequately expresses it is the basic power of love, and this is without measure."[34] Here the word 'love' refers to our spiritual dynamism that drives us out of ourselves in an unlimited movement toward the infinite good which is perceived as personal. Of course, this transcendental love is always mediated by encounters with other human beings, but this only highlights its measureless character. Human love, as we experience it, involves a desire to effect the good of the other through a reaching out to other persons in their uniqueness. However, since this occurs within the movement toward the absolute good, every loving relationship falls short of the ideal. Lovers can never say they love enough, and the beloved is never able to respond totally. Love, as we experience it, is indeed without measure, because the lover desires the absolute good which is always beyond grasp.

To substantiate the claim that love is the "only ultimate structure of the person," we must examine more closely the relationship between knowledge and love since these are the two fundamental powers of human beings. The finite spirit achieves itself in its union with the world of persons and things. When this world is intentionally brought into the person, we have knowledge; and when the person reaches out to other persons in their uniqueness and for their own sake, we have love. In one sense, love has a primacy since it attains to others in themselves, while knowledge reaches them only as present in the knower. However, love and knowledge should be thought of, not as two totally separate human operations, but as constituting together the one basic disposition of the human being. "The more I know the other personally, the more I can love him. The more I love him, the better I understand him. This is so because of the ultimate unity of knowing and willing in the free self-actuation of the spirit."[35] In this light an analysis of human transcendence which restricts itself to the cognitive realm appears incomplete. Human beings are, not simply objective observers drinking in facts about their world, but persons whose genuine knowing is always shaped by volitional elements. From the very beginning our transcendence involves freedom since we are called upon to accept freely our dependence on a power outside of ourselves. This fundamental structure is manifested in our everyday life, where our loves determine our perceptions of the world. Knowledge always has a volitional aspect since in the questioning which leads to knowledge there is always present a desire to know and a striving to know more. In addition, our deeper modes of knowing involve personal participation, involvement, and commitment.[36] Without love, knowledge is in danger of becoming merely a means of manipulation and control which fosters the eclipse of mystery.

Only love allows us to appreciate the riches of our world and to achieve a deeper self-understanding. This point implies that we can only move toward a proper understanding of the absolute good, which supports and draws our freedom, by loving this mystery. It is not as though we first came to a neutral, objective knowledge of the mystery and then decided whether or not we should love it. Only a loving commitment to the absolute mystery that surrounds us can reveal it to us as a gracious good which supports and justifies our original commitment. By stressing the volitional element we see human transcendentality as striving for the good as well as the truth, as requiring commitment as well as objectivity, as involving reaching out as well as return to self. If we use the word 'love' to describe this dynamism and remember that it always includes a cognitive element, then we can say with justification that love is the fundamental structure of the human person.

Now out of this analysis of transcendental freedom as the basis of choice and love we can arrive at certain existentials or ontological structures found in human existence.

(a) Human freedom is intelligible only on condition that persons are finite spirits. We must be spirit because we are able to take a stand in relation to being itself, we achieve a degree of self-possession and self-understanding, we transcend the particularities of our existence, we decide about ourselves as a whole, and we are able to choose among particular goods. However, at the same time we must be finite because we do not possess being itself but must decide about it, our fundamental attitude toward ourselves can be changed, our love is never complete, and we only gradually move toward a total self-possession which we never achieve.

(b) The fact that human beings must necessarily take up an attitude toward their contingent existence shows that they are personal subjects.[37] We are, not simply a series of disparate free acts strung together, but unified, enduring selves. We do not merely choose this or that but create the kind of person we will be. We are not merely products of determined necessities but are responsible for our lives in their entirety. In choosing between various particular goods persons experience themselves as distinct from and standing over against each one of them. Thus, it can be said that human freedom is intelligible only on condition that we are personal subjects who, as unified selves, transcend the particularities of our situation.

(c) There is a fundamental fissure within the human being which can be described in terms of a split between person and nature.[38] We are "person" insofar as we freely dispose of ourselves and incorporate various aspects of our existence into our fundamental option; "nature" refers to all the elements in us which are given prior to free decision or which escape the integrating power of freedom. This kind of structure must be posited in human beings as the condition of possibility for the fact that we cannot achieve total self-acceptance, that our fundamental attitude toward ourselves only gradually (and never totally) extends to all segments of our existence, that we are not able to gather ourselves totally in one decisive act, and that our love remains mixed with selfishness. Many imbalances and contradictions experienced in life can be traced to this fundamental self-alienation in which humans as persons cannot integrate all the "givens" of their existence.[39]

(d) Materiality is the a priori condition for the conflict within finite freedom between person and nature. Since human beings cannot achieve total self-possession or complete self-giving, even though they are spirit, we must posit in them a metaphysical principle which impedes the normal operation of spirit. We can call this principle "materiality" and posit it as the condition which accounts for the fundamental split in human freedom. Human freedom is incomplete because we are material beings.

(e) Human freedom in all its ambiguity is intelligible only on condition that we are beings threatened by sin and guilt.[40] Our freedom is always exercised in a world codetermined by guilt. The situations and material presented to our freedom are the product of a history which, from the very beginning, has been created in part by sin. While we can transcend the sinful element by refusing to ratify it in our decisions, we cannot avoid encountering it and freely taking up an attitude toward it. The threat to freedom also comes from within. We can refuse to accept our creaturehood and contradict our transcendentality by a rejection of its point of orientation. Our loves or ultimate concerns can be out of tune with the actual structure of reality. Individual free decisions can contradict our fundamental option. In all of these ways human freedom is revealed as it is actually experienced: threatened by sin and guilt. We are indeed beings subject to the mystery of evil.

In trying to uncover our ontological structures through an analysis of freedom, it becomes clear that we are not a static human nature enclosed upon itself but that we are in process of creating ourselves through our free choices. It could be said that our essence is precisely that we do not have a fixed essence but are fundamentally open to the transcendent, a condition which in turn gives us the unavoidable responsibility of determining our very being. Part of the significance of this insight is that it keeps us from a reified, static understanding of all of the essential characteristics of human existence.

Having noted these various characteristics of human existence, we should now make explicit the fact that they are all rooted in our essential nature as openness to absolute mystery. Human beings must be characterized as finite spirit because their love tends toward the mystery (conceived as the absolute good) without ever being able to comprehend it. Our personal subjectivity is rooted in the fact that in our exercise of freedom we transcend all particulars and ratify or reject our necessary relation to the mysterious source of our life. All of our characteristics which express limitation (nature, materiality, alienation through sin and guilt) are inferred from our experience of striving for the absolute mystery without being able to grasp it or definitively choose it. In summary, freedom as we know it is only possible if human beings are spiritual, personal subjects who, in their effort to affirm the absolute mystery, are at the same time finite, material, and radically threatened.

At the conclusion of our second model on freedom, the importance of understanding the models as dialectically related should be noted. Our discussions of questioning and freedom should be viewed as complementary: only taken together do they give us a balanced understanding of human transcendentality. The cognitive and volitional aspects must both be included: we are knowers and lovers, we question and are free, we seek the absolute truth and the absolute good, we are self-present and self-giving. These aspects are not simply set side by side in us but mutually condition one another and flow from a primordial unified source. Our deepest responses issue from our unique personal subjectivity and include cognitive and affective elements joined in an inseparable unity. Love is the "light of knowledge" and knowledge is "the luminous radiance of love."[41]

CHAPTER EIGHT

Mystery Vindicated

NOW THAT WE HAVE shown that an analysis of human experience suggests the presence of mystery, we must investigate the truth claims implicitly present in our models. Effective mystagogues not only disclose mystery but must also defend their claims. To proceed in orderly fashion we will clarify the exact nature of the claims, determine the appropriate ways of vindicating them, and finally present both direct and indirect arguments in their defense.

I. THE CLAIMS

We took as our aim in presenting the models the disclosure of mystery. It was a matter of trying to bring to conscious awareness a dimension of existence that in our modern world often lies hidden. The ideal was to construct coherent models which could thematize this realm of mystery in a meaningful way. The hope was that the phenomenology would be convincing in the sense of striking responsive chords in the readers so that they would identify with the descriptions and discover transcendence in their own experience. In addition, the ontological considerations were designed to reinforce and universalize the perception of mystery by rooting it in the essential structures of human existence. Hence, the models would be considered successful if they produced the conviction that experience indeed does point to a realm beyond scientific investigation which we can aptly call "mystery." At this point the next logical question is, Does such a dimension actually exist or not? The talk of mystery rings bells and lights up experience, but is it true? Does it point to some existing reality? The models promote self-awareness, but is this a mere subjectivism? We are indeed pointed to a transcendental realm, but is this merely a projection or an illusion?

In all these ways a mystagogy could be heard as meaningful,

but the question of its claim to truth would remain. This question could be posed in a number of ways: Is there an existing referent for human transcendentality? Is the scope of our dynamic spirit finite or infinite? Is there an actual source and goal for the finite human spirit? Is there an absolute truth which motivates our infinite questioning? Does an infinite good actually exist which grounds our freedom? Will our longings for perfect love find a real fulfillment? Is there an actually existing infinite horizon which is the condition for all our human experience? Is a religious interpretation of existence justified? In short, we are asking whether the mystery we have disclosed actually exists. Of course, throughout our treatment the implicit claim has been that it does, and now we must try to justify or validate that position.

In fact, the models have claimed more than this. They have been slanted toward a positive interpretation of human experience, one which understands the mystery as gracious. This was highlighted in the discussion of freedom in which the infinite horizon was viewed as the absolute good, and the assertion was made that only a loving personal commitment to this mystery would reveal its graciousness. Thus, we are dealing with a further claim that can be expressed in various ways: the source of life can be trusted, life is meaningful rather than absurd, our longings will be fulfilled rather than eternally frustrated, the goal lovingly draws us, and a theistic interpretation of experience is justified. In short, the contention is that the mystery disclosed by the mystagogical models not only exists but is gracious.

Perhaps we can clarify this matter by placing it in the larger context of Christian apologetics.[1] A complete defense of Christian claims involves at least three distinct questions. Is a religious interpretation of our experience meaningful and true? Is a theistic interpretation meaningful and true? Is a christological explanation meaningful and true?[2] This suggests that an apologist must first establish the fact that an understanding of human existence which posits the presence of transcendence (or ultimacy, mystery, limit, etc.) is both meaningful in the sense of disclosing and thematizing an authentic aspect of common experience and true in the sense of being a universal and necessary condition for all experience.[3] Then it must be shown that the referent implied in a religious interpretation can be understood on the theistic model provided by the Christian tradition. This would include explicating the Christian understanding of God in coherent conceptual language showing that it is adequate to our experience, and attempting to validate its truth claims through a metaphysical or transcendental analysis. Finally, there must be an effort to justify the contention that the story of Jesus can best illumine our experience and that God has actually revealed himself in Jesus as the absolute mediator of salvation.

Let us try to locate our own effort within this framework. Some points are clear: the models have already attempted to show that a religious interpretation of experience in terms of mystery is meaningful, the task of demonstrating the truth claim of this religious interpretation still faces us, and the whole christological question is clearly beyond the scope of this book. When we get to the theistic position the matter is not so easy. Our assertion has been that the mystery disclosed in the models is gracious. Now it seems that this can be taken as some type of theistic claim. If the mystery is gracious, it is personal and can be called the "holy mystery" or "God." However, this theism cannot be equated with a full-blown Christian understanding of God, and it is important not to slide too easily from gracious mystery to the God of the New Testament.[4] Therefore, our task is to justify a limited theistic assertion. Concretely, this means that we will bypass the question of the attributes of God and the recent discussion on reinterpreting the doctrine of God[5] but will treat the so-called "proofs" for God's existence. I do not think that the problems of the proofs and of reinterpreting doctrine are totally dichotomous, but a separation for our purposes seems legitimate. Therefore, in this chapter we want to validate the claim that religious and theistic interpretations of human experience not only are meaningful (as indicated by our models) but are also true. To express this in other terms, we want to vindicate the assertion that the source and goal of human transcendentality is an actually existing gracious mystery.

II. THE APPROACH

It seems that there are two general approaches that can be followed in trying to vindicate the cognitive claims involved in religious and theistic interpretations of life: one direct and the other indirect.

1. The direct approach involves metaphysics, that is, the science which investigates the foundations of all reality and searches out what is common to all beings. In modern times this general task of metaphysics has often been carried out by an explicit transcendental method which looks for the necessary and the universal

through an analysis of the a priori structures which make the activity of the human subject possible.[6] We have already employed a transcendental method in order to discover the ontological structures which ground human spiritual activity. Now we want to use it to vindicate the assertion that human experience demands absolute mystery as the condition of its possibility.

A major problem with this approach is the general distrust of metaphysics today. To overcome this, it might help to point out the constructive role that metaphysical analysis plays within process theology.[7] One could also note a growing openness to some type of metaphysical thought within the analytic tradition.[8] Finally, we could note a certain optimism about the possibilities of philosophical theology which can be found in thinkers representing various traditions.[9] However, rather than pursue these points or try to mount a full-scale defense of metaphysics, we will presuppose the general principle that as we probe our experience, philosophical reflection is unavoidable (the only question being whether it is done explicitly and therefore self-critically, or implicitly and thus uncritically) and that a transcendental method of some sort is necessary since there is always a subjective factor in our knowing.[10]

In defending the use of metaphysics special problems arise when we consider the proofs for God's existence since they are (in their traditional form) so widely discredited today.[11] The ontological argument of Anselm has been attacked as an illicit jump from the world of ideas to reality, and the "five ways" of Aquinas have been denounced as an unjustified leap from finite experience to the infinite. Furthermore, the very effort to demonstrate or prove God's existence is seen by some as a failure to appreciate human finitude and God's transcendence.

In this situation it is important to specify the precise role that philosophical analysis is to play in dealing with the question of the existence of God. First, we should note some commonly accepted limitations. Hans Küng summarizes them in this way: it is not possible to prove God's existence by a detached, objective, rational demonstration; there is no single proof that is generally acceptable; and there is no combination of proofs that is actually convincing to everyone.[12] However, even if we accept this appraisal, we cannot simply give up the effort to show the reasonableness of faith; other options must be explored. For example, we could envision a new style of philosophical theology which would begin with an examination of the believer's basic convictions (those which precede and enable the acceptance of any formal proof) and attempt to discover the conditions that could make these convictions valid and reasonable.[13] We could also think of reason's role as one of vindicating a theistic position (as opposed to demonstrating it from agreed premises) by showing that the very act of denying God's existence contains an implicit affirmation of it.[14] Rahner suggests another option when he describes the proofs as an attempt to bring to reflexive awareness man's necessary relationship to the absolute mystery which is always present even when suppressed or denied.[15] This means that the proofs are meant, not to demonstrate some new objective knowledge about a being previously unknown, but to call attention to a reality that is already co-known. An important element in Rahner's approach (as well as for Macquarrie, Donceel, and others) is the existential involvement of the inquirer in the question. For example, the proofs take on meaning when individuals are struggling to understand their deeper experiences or when someone feels the need to justify fundamental personal convictions. This is because the truth claimed by theism is not restricted to objective propositions, but involves an enlightened self-understanding which is adequate to the full range of experience. In short, an appreciation of the proofs demands involvement rather than detachment.

While it may be well to avoid the phrase "proofs for the existence of God," we can make use of the metaphysical style of analysis implied in these optional approaches. This means employing a transcendental method in order to justify the religious claim that the absolute mystery must be posited as a condition which makes human spiritual activity possible, and attempting to work out a philosophical defense of the truth claims of theism. In doing so we should keep in mind the limitations of reason, the challenges to the traditional proofs, and the priority of lived experience over rational reflection.

2. The great difficulty in coming up with acceptable direct proofs for theistic claims forces us to look for an alternate approach. We can find guidance by examining Rahner's search for an indirect justification of the Christian faith which will be intellectually honest but will bypass certain individual points of controversy in an effort to achieve a type of certitude about faith as a whole.[16] He calls this activity a "first level of reflection" and compares it to the "illative sense" of Cardinal Newman which he interprets as providing (through a convergence of probabilities) an initial certitude about decisions which affect the self as a whole. In this first level of reflection the task is to reflect systematically upon human beings as the ones who call themselves as a whole into question and upon Christianity as a response to this question. To accomplish this, we need a close con-

nection between fundamental and dogmatic theology in which the
very content of particular Christian doctrines becomes an important
element in the proof. In other words, doctrines are credible precisely
because they are seen as coherent responses to the question we are
and as articulations of convictions and longings already possessed.

This indirect method involves a type of coherence theory of
truth in which the criterion is whether a particular insight or proposition faithfully illumines and accounts for our experience.[17] More specifically, the criteria which are implicit in it are similar to the ones
adduced by John Macquarrie for judging the truth claims of theological statements: that they express a "unifying vision" which "constitutes
a harmonious whole and leaves out nothing of importance in the
range of human experience," that they are not at variance with other
well-founded beliefs, and that they are open to further development.[18] In a coherence theory of truth a good phenomenology is
already a major step toward validating a particular claim.[19] A good
descriptive analysis is convincing precisely because it gives us a unified
picture that accounts for our experience. We recognize the patterns
and structures revealed as our own. The picture appears correct because it encompasses and integrates what we value and believe. Thus,
a good phenomenology can move us to judge its assertions not only
meaningful but true.

There are also certain affinities between the indirect method
and a pragmatic theory of truth. It is a matter of determining if a
particular world view or interpretive scheme does a better job not
only of interpreting the deeper experience of life but also of enabling
a person to live with greater freedom and nobility. Hence, one of the
criteria for truth is the very pragmatic one of better living—an appealing approach to those who attach greater importance to lived
experience than reflection. The indirect method is interested in validating a religious and theistic life-style as a whole, without having to
give a theoretical scientific justification for all the presuppositions
involved in it. This brings us close to a pragmatic view of truth which
insists that "the fundamental criterion of truth lies in the fruitful
consequences which follow from an idea or judgment."[20] The real
significance of this method is that it provides an intellectually honest
way of validating faith when a scientific metaphysical proof is in practice impossible. Thus, it provides a second general method of validating the truth claims implicit in our models by looking at the view of
human life based on the presence of a gracious mystery and seeing if
in comparison with other options it is not a more coherent, faithful,
and helpful explanation of our experience.

III. THE DIRECT APPROACH

1. Let us begin with the religious claim that human activity demands the existence of the infinite as the condition of its possibility. As we noted, this assertion can be expressed in a number of ways: there is a transcendent dimension in human experience, the scope of our spiritual dynamism is infinite, the goal of human transcendentality is absolute being. This thesis can, of course, be denied by claiming that speculative reason cannot get beyond the phenomenal world and that objective judgments simply involve the synthesis of sense data. Thus Immanuel Kant, the classic proponent of this position, in concluding his discussion of space and time as subjective conditions which help explain how this synthesis is accomplished, writes:

> When in *a priori* judgment we seek to go out beyond the given concept, we come in the *a priori* intuitions upon that which cannot be discovered in the concept but which is certainly found *a priori* in the intuition corresponding to the concept, and can be connected with it synthetically. Such judgments, however, thus based on intuition, can never extend beyond objects of the senses; they are valid only for objects of possible experience.[21]

It is true that Kant admits there is an idea of God, a supreme Ideal, which helps man organize his thinking (a merely regulative function), but he denies that speculative reason can affirm its existence or, in other words, grant it a constitutive function.[22] The religious claim could also be denied by asserting that the object of human striving is not the infinite but the indefinite.[23] This would mean that one recognizes the dynamism of the knowing process but claims that it has no final end. In other words, the knower is motivated by the desire to gain more and more knowledge, but not a completely satisfying final object. Finally, we could add to the list of objectors all those who hold total reductionist, empiricist, or positivist views as well as those who in practical living make an absolute out of science or technology.

Rather than attacking these objections directly, we will first respond by offering a metaphysical vindication of the claim that human knowing implies not only the possibility but the actual existence of the infinite. In doing so we must presume the phenomenology of questioning found in the previous chapter as well as the metaphysical anthropology which viewed persons as finite spirits immersed in a material world. In other words, we have already accomplished the reductive phase of the transcendental method by establishing the conditions in human beings which make knowing possible; now we can presume those results as we pursue the deductive phase which attempts to uncover the structures of reality in general.[24]

Let us begin the vindication by looking again at the process of abstraction by which we attain universal concepts.[25] Human knowledge is not restricted to individual items of experience; on the contrary, we are able to attain concepts which can be applied to many singulars.[26] This cannot be explained as a process of generalizing from individual instances since we often attain these concepts from a very limited sampling. Nor should it be understood as the detaching and impressing of a spiritual image on the mind. Rather, abstraction really involves the ability to recognize that a particular form is not exhausted in an individual, sensible manifestation but is open to further realizations of itself. In other words, it is the power to know the sensibly intuited as limited. However, this is possible only if the knower already, in some way, has an anticipatory knowledge of the potential for further realization possessed by the form. It cannot be recognized as limited unless there is some perception of its further possibilities. The problem is to determine the scope or horizon of this preapprehension. It cannot be a particular object since all objects are recognized as limited only within a larger horizon. It is not limited to sense data because the positing of such a limitation already indicates we are beyond it, since we only know limitation in terms of a larger whole. It is not "nothingness": first of all, because privations are known only in relation to an actual fullness; and second, because in gaining knowledge the knower is actualized, which indicates that the ultimate object of knowing is act as opposed to empty nothingness. We are left with the position that the goal of human transcendence is *esse:* the in-itself unlimited act of all beings.[27] *Esse* is the fullest of notions, the ground of all the determinations of an existent, that which brings the form or essence to actuality. It is only in a preapprehension of absolute *esse* that the knower is able to recognize the form of every sensible singular as limited and as open to further realizations. No finite object can fill the horizon of the human spirit, and for that very reason it is recognized as limited. In short, abstraction as we know it is possible only on condition of the presence of absolute *esse* as the infinite horizon for our knowing.

We can continue our vindication by examining judgment. Our knowing is characterized by an unlimited striving for further knowledge.[28] In the midst of this striving we attain particular items of knowledge or truth through judgments. Now it is important to examine not only the content or results of judgment (as Kant did) but also the process or activity of judging. There are really two forms of judgment: the synthetic, which unifies concepts, and the objective or affirmative, in which the synthesis is referred to reality. This affirmation of a particular truth is intelligible only in terms of a movement toward a final infinite end.[29] The very drive to affirm particular truths flows from our radical desire for truth itself. Each achievement of knowledge is never totally satisfying and only leads to a further desire to know. In every judgment we stand over against a particular object and are able to view it as only a limited realization of the drive for absolute truth. Joseph Maréchal offers us this summary of the argument:

> Thus we are induced to postulate in our objective knowledge something more than the static reception and the abstractive analysis of 'data,' a movement of thought which would bring us constantly 'beyond' that which may still be represented by concepts, some kind of metempirical anticipation which should show us the objective capacity of our intellect expanding infinitely until it exceeds any limitation of being. Otherwise there can be no analogical knowledge of the transcendent. Hence in order to explain and safeguard the latter we are induced to take our stand on the domain of the *dynamic finality* of our spirit. For only an 'internal finality' of the intellect may make it constantly exceed the present object and strive infinitely towards a wider object.[30]

The third way of developing the main thesis that the infinite is implied in human knowing is by an examination of questioning.[31] Human questioning moves beyond every particular question and aims ultimately at the questionable itself, or the totality of all that can be questioned. The questionable itself is unlimited since we can always call into question any supposed limits. Since we are able to ask about the totality of the questionable, we must posit a unified aspect under which we inquire about all particular beings. The only possible common element is *esse:* the act by which individual things are able to exist. Since everything is questioned under this aspect, we can say that the human questioner must have some type of awareness of *esse* as a condition of possibility for all his questioning. It is known, not as an object or as the sum total of particular objects, but as the framework within which all particular knowledge occurs. Now we must determine the scope or extent of this *esse*. We desire to know about *esse* not merely as it relates to our own interests but also as it is in itself. If someone would say he is interested in *esse* in a limited way, he would have already surpassed the limit because a limit can be known only in relation to a larger horizon. Therefore, we can say that the horizon of our ability to question everything is itself absolute and unconditioned. Since we already identified *esse* with this horizon, it follows that our questioning implies absolute *esse* as a condition of its possibility.[32]

I think that the full force of these three arguments can only be appreciated when they are seen in the framework of the metaphysics of knowledge from which they flow. There can be no question here of explaining such a comprehensive theory, but it may help if we treat briefly two of its essential premises as they are developed by Rahner.[33] The first is that being and knowing are convertible.[34] He argues that if we can ask about being in its totality, then we are affirming its fundamental knowability.[35] We cannot ask about what is totally unknown. But this close relationship must be rooted in a primordial unity of being and knowing; otherwise we cannot account for their actual unity in the knowing process. This leads us to the second premise: knowing is self-presence. If being and knowing form a primordial unity, then knowing cannot be explained on the model of a camera taking a picture because the original unity precludes this kind of separation. Rather, it is a matter of increased self-awareness which results when knowers, who are already united with the material world, achieve a return to self which allows them to recognize the limitations of the intuited sensible object (abstraction) and gives them the distance to make judgments about reality. In short, knowing occurs only through self-presence. Rahner summarizes all of this in the general principle: "Knowing is the being-present-to-self of being, and this being-present-to-self is the being of the existent."[36] The key to understanding this principle is to realize that it defines knowing in terms of its highest manifestation. There are degrees of intensity of being which are determined by the ability to return to self. Human knowers, limited by materiality, cannot achieve a complete return to self, and thus the complete identification of being and knowing cannot be achieved. Human knowing is a deficient mode of the highest type of knowing which must involve total self-presence and the complete identification of absolute being and knowing. Therefore, the fact that human knowing is limited does not vitiate the principle but exemplifies the notion that it is operative according to the degree of being possessed by the knower.

In the light of these principles the argument against the Kantian insistence on a merely regulative role for the absolute becomes

clearer. If being and knowing are originally united, then it is difficult to divorce them in the act of knowing. The ontological structure
of the knower and that which grounds his knowing ability must be
common. The questing spirit in its drive to understand reality is
already in touch with being itself. The *esse* which is the object of
human transcendence cannot arbitrarily be excluded from the realm
of existing being and reduced to a regulative ideal. In short, it is
really a question, not of whether knowing can reach being in itself or
not, but of a knowing which is possible only on condition that absolute being is always already present.

If we recall that the return to self which knowing involves is at
the same time a self-transcendence, we can establish the actual existence of the infinite from this angle as well.[37] We experience our
knowing both as self-awareness and as a reaching beyond ourselves, a
dynamic drive which surpasses all particulars in a movement toward
the infinite. Now this infinite cannot be a creation of human beings
since it is precisely that which makes the dynamic activity of the
knower possible. The infinite is known (or better, co-known) precisely
in the act of self-transcendence, not as a subsequent deduction from
singulars. Therefore, we must say that an existing infinite must be
posited as the condition of possibility for the whole process of knowing. If persons were not self-present, they could escape from this
necessary, if implicit, affirmation of absolute being. However, this is
impossible since even an attempt to deny this thesis demands self-
presence as a condition of its possibility. Therefore the objectors,
since they are necessarily self-present, are involved in the contradiction of denying what they implicitly affirm in the act of denial, that is,
the presence of the infinite as a condition for their self-presence.

In summary, we have argued that within a Rahnerian metaphysics of knowledge it is possible to work out a cogent vindication
of the religious claim by showing that an actual absolute or infinite
must be posited as the condition for human knowing viewed specifically as abstraction, judgment, and questioning.

2. In moving from a religious to a limited theistic assertion the
problem is one of getting from mystery to gracious mystery, from
the absolute to the absolute good, from being in general to the
absolute being called "God." In other words, we presuppose the
vindication of the religious claim and must now show that the infinite can legitimately be characterized as benign. Let us explore some
ways of accomplishing this.

We can repeat the formal structure of the argument based on
knowing and place it in the context of freedom. In this perspective

we view human transcendentality not only as intentional but as valuational, that is, as involving great existential interest and aiming at the highest good. Again, we presume a phenomenology which reveals persons as individuals who necessarily take up an attitude toward their contingent existence and thereby affirm or deny the ground of this existence. Human existence is clearly dependent on a source outside ourselves which must possess existence itself since no cause can give what it does not have. Now we are called upon to adopt a positive attitude toward our existence, or else we place ourselves in an ultimate contradiction. The only firm basis for making such a positive affirmation is that the source of life can be trusted. Therefore, the demand to accept one's contingent existence is only intelligible on the condition that the ultimate source is gracious. This line of argumentation would have to be completed by retorsion if someone claimed that this demand was simply absurd. We could say, for example, that the very effort to argue the point presupposes a limited meaning which itself must be grounded in a context of ultimate meaning. Once we grant meaning to the fact that we must necessarily affirm our contingent existence, then we are back to affirming gracious mystery as the only condition that makes such a free action possible and intelligible.

It is also possible to argue from freedom of choice to the existence of the absolute good. The fact that we can choose freely is based on our ability to recognize particular realities as merely limited goods.[38] But something can be recognized as a partial good only in relation to the absolute good. Therefore, we must affirm the existence of this absolute good as a condition which makes free choice possible. The claim that the highest good must exist can be reinforced by showing that the existence of partial goods demands it and that its denial would contradict the fundamental unity of being and knowing.

While we have only briefly outlined the arguments based on freedom (presuming many points previously established), one advantage is clear: they conclude to a gracious source and absolute good which brings us closer (than infinite or absolute, for example) to what we commonly mean by "God."

As we noted previously, the argument based on questioning concludes to the existence of the unconditioned or infinite. Does this amount to a demonstration of God's existence? Coreth, who has so carefully developed the argument based on questioning, says it does not.[39] It concludes to the existence of *esse* in general and not to the absolute being as the transcendent cause of all particular beings. To vindicate a theistic claim requires further argumentation. It must be shown that the questioners themselves are necessarily finite because they cannot completely grasp the infinite and do not possess their own being absolutely. As finite they are not being itself and are distinct from absolute being. Since, however, there is a necessity about our actual existence (i.e., we cannot just stop existing), our existence must be based on an absolute being which possesses its own being and exists necessarily in an absolute sense. We call this absolute transcendent cause "God." We should note the structure of the argument. It does not begin by presupposing a finite contingent being and then go from the contingent to the necessary. Instead, it starts by establishing the unconditioned nature of the goal of human questioning, then demonstrates the finite character of the questioner, and, finally, shows that the absolute being (God) must be posited as a condition which makes our finite existence possible.

Let us try to make the step from a religious to a theistic position in still another way.[40] Human knowers recognize the limitation of everything they know. But this implies that they are already beyond every finite limit through their unlimited desire to know, since they cannot know something as limited unless they are somehow beyond this limit. It is not just a matter of surpassing this or that particular limit, but it is limit as such which the knower seeks to transcend. In doing so, we implicitly affirm the infinite as the goal of our striving. However, can we say that this infinite goal exists as a meaningful term for human transcendence? If it does not, then we must posit a contradiction in the very core of human existence, for we then strive naturally and unavoidably for something which it is impossible to attain. If, however, life has meaning, then this is an untenable position, and we are forced to posit an existing infinite (God) which satisfies human longings. The crucial part of the argument is the assumption that life has real meaning. For those who deny this a retorsive argument must be employed which shows that their human activity (arguing this point, for example) implicitly affirms the meaning of life which they are explicitly denying. In conclusion, we can note that the formal structure of this vindication is to articulate the desire for the infinite and then to argue that the denial of its existence puts one in fundamental contradiction.

Finally, it is possible to move from a religious to a theistic position by simply identifying infinite, absolute, highest good, mystery, gracious mystery, and God; or (to state the point more cautiously) by claiming that a proof for God's existence is not dependent on precisely distinguishing them.[41] In this approach there is only one proof for God's existence: that human transcendence demands mystery as its condition of possibility. All variants simply begin with different manifestations of our essential transcendence and conclude to various designations of the one absolute mystery. It is not essential to the argument to distinguish the ways we describe the goal of our transcendence.[42]

This approach begins by describing concrete human experience (for example, knowing and willing or whatever experience is most available for analysis in depth) and tries to show that it is intelligible only if we posit an infinite source and term for this experience. However, this reflexive awareness of human striving and its infinite dimension is only a limited perception of our original, fundamental, abiding orientation to absolute mystery. In other words, there is a primordial knowing and loving which is always richer and deeper than any explicit awareness of it and which can only be understood in relation to an infinite source and goal. This approach places the attempt to vindicate a theistic claim into a participative context. It is, not a matter of a neutral search for a particular objective reality called "God," but rather an effort to articulate in ever-clearer terms the deep, often hidden, but unavoidable experience of mystery. The success of this process seems to rest on the quality of the descriptions of human transcendence (Are they convincing?), on the validity of the claim that mystery is the term of human transcendentality, and on a coherent explanation of this orienting term.

We have already discussed the first two points, and now it will be helpful to examine at length the way Rahner develops the third. In general he uses his fundamental principle of the primordial unity of being and knowing to establish that the goal of transcendence cannot be a projection but must really exist. Thus, we ourselves cannot create this goal because it is the enabling condition for all our activity in the first place. From there he goes on to specify the goal of transcendence more precisely. In doing so he recognizes that there are philosophical problems involved but takes the position (at least in *Foundations*) that we must proceed even though they are not solved. In this regard he writes:

> The philosopher might give further reflection especially to the question of how a transcendental relationship to what he calls being, and a transcendental relationship to God are related and how they are to be distinguished.
>
> Since we want to consider directly only the original, transcendental knowledge of God, which is antecedent to and is not able to be recaptured completely by reflexive ontology, we can

take a shorter, although to be sure less cautious, route here, because the hesitant caution of philosophy cannot become a substitute for risking an understanding of existence which is always prior to philosophy.[43]

Following this "less cautious route," he goes on to describe the goal as infinite, indefinable, ineffable, and finally as holy mystery. He justifies the characterization "holy" by analyzing human freedom and love. They demand as a condition of their possibility an absolute mystery which is not at our disposal but which opens up our transcendence. Since this absolute mystery is beyond human control and yet grounds our ability to love freely, it must be gracious and can be aptly named "holy mystery."

However, there remain serious problems with this approach.[44] For one thing it admittedly leaves unresolved the relationship between the goal *(esse)* of our spiritual striving and the infinite God proclaimed by Christians. As a matter of fact, it is possible to discern two opposing lines of thought in Rahner's writings. One suggests that the object of human transcendence is somehow limited and therefore cannot be identified with God. Thus he writes:

> Hence, insofar as this *esse* simultaneously apprehended in the pre-apprehension is able to be limited, it shows itself to be non-absolute, since an absolute necessarily excludes the possibility of a limitation. This *esse* apprehended in the pre-apprehension is therefore in itself *esse 'commune'* ('common' *esse*), although this must not be equated with *ens commune.*[45]

The second line of thought claims that God himself is co-affirmed by our spiritual dynamism:

> But in this pre-apprehension as the necessary and always already realized condition of knowledge (even in a doubt, an in-itself, and thus *esse* is affirmed) the existence of an Absolute Being is also affirmed simultaneously *(mitbejaht)*. For any possible object which can come to exist in the breadth of the pre-apprehension is simultaneously affirmed. An Absolute Being would completely fill up the breadth of this pre-apprehension. Hence it is simultaneously affirmed as real (since it cannot be grasped as merely possible). In this sense, but only in this sense, it can be said: the pre-apprehension attains to God.[46]

How are we to reconcile these two opposing positions? Vincent Branick has suggested that there are really two moments or directions in human striving.[47] One aims at *esse commune,* which, although it is unlimited in itself, is limited as the act of the essence of particular beings. The other aims at *esse absolutum,* which is in fact infinite and can be called "God." This explanation is helpful in the sense of further specifying the two aspects of Rahner's thought, but it is not really a solution to the problem since it leaves unclarified the primordial relationship between *esse commune* and *esse absolutum* and takes the unacceptable position that somehow human transcendentality has two separate terms.

My position is that Rahner did not really succeed in solving the problem on a philosophical level in his early works and has abandoned any effort to do so in his subsequent writings. Without solving the speculative problem he opts for the practical solution of speaking of a single unified goal for human transcendence which can be specified as *esse commune, esse absolutum,* holy mystery, and God. The core of the unsolved philosophical issue is this: If there is one goal *(esse)* of human transcendentality, how can it remain absolute and unlimited and still be the act of particular beings which implies limitation? It seems to me that the problem really arises from the fear of positing any change in God as *esse absolutum.* The presupposition is that any real involvement with finite beings means change in the absolute being which in turn implies imperfection. If the problem is framed in this way, I believe there are resources in the Rahnerian corpus for dealing with it.[48] In a theological context he writes:

> God can become something, he who is unchangeable in himself can *himself* become subject to change *in something else.* . . . But this 'changing *in* another must neither be taken as denying the immutability of God in himself nor simply be reduced to a changement *of* the other. Here ontology has to orientate itself according to the message of faith and not try to lecture it . . . *he* can truly *become* something. . . . And this possibility is not a sign of deficiency, but the height of his perfection, which would be less if in addition to being infinite, he could not become less than he (always) is.[49]

This theological insight suggests that the general relationship between absolute and finite being could be worked out in the more dynamic terms of mutual conditioning.[50]

Following this suggestion, we could say that absolute *esse* as the object of human transcendence really changes in the other (as the act of its existence) without denying its immutability or its perfection. The one *esse* is both absolute and common. The key to my solution is the perception that the root of the traditional problem as Rahner grappled with it is the fear of being forced to posit change and imperfection in God. If we can judge involvement, relationship, becoming, and immanence to be perfections, as the process thinkers stress, and as Rahner has on occasion admitted, then the way is clear for allowing *esse absolutum* to function as the formal cause of the existence of all finite beings.[51] Granting this solution, we then have a legitimate philosophical basis for proceeding from the infinite to the absolute being and from a religious claim to a theistic one.

Now that we have sketched out various ways of establishing a theistic position, let us examine some of their characteristic features.[52]

(a) They are not demonstrations, but vindications. A strict demonstration begins with agreed premises and argues syllogistically to a logical conclusion. In our case one of the premises cannot achieve an initial agreement since it is precisely the point at issue: that the existence of God is implied in particular acts of questioning, willing, and knowing. In this situation we make use of a retorsive argument which tries to show that an explicit verbal denial of the thesis involves an implicit affirmation of it. In other words, the person who says God does not exist is involved in a contradiction since this very affirmation is an act which implicitly affirms an infinite horizon as the condition of its possibility. Hence, through this retorsive argument a theistic position is vindicated rather than demonstrated. Finally, it bears repeating that the contradiction is, not between concepts, but between a verbalized position and what is implicit in a particular action such as questioning, willing, loving, or knowing.

(b) In the vindications God is not attained as an object but is co-known as the source and term of some aspect of human transcendentality. When we speak about God, we are involved in a categorical or secondary knowledge of him which is possible only within the horizon of a more original and deeper transcendental awareness of the absolute being. Hence, all explicit theistic arguments in order to be true to their nature must point back to the absolute mystery which grounds human transcendentality. Since God is known as the background or horizon of our knowing rather than as its object, we must recognize the limitations of our ability to speak about him. No proof or vindication comprehends what God is in himself, or even what we experience of him at a transcendental level. Their purpose is rather to point to or illumine this deeper level of awareness. All of this helps us gain perspective on the limited goals of our theistic vindications and serves as a response to those who feel that philosophical argumentation calls God's transcendence into question.

(c) The vindications are based on the principle of final causality rather than efficient causality. The traditional proofs were often interpreted as proceeding from known effects to an infinite cause by way of the principle of efficient causality. This principle in turn was seen as a generalization of the laws of nature in which every effect must have a proportionate cause. The more contemporary vindications argue rather that God is known as the goal and motivating source of all aspects of human transcendence. The principle at work is: "Whatever is not intelligible by itself, is intelligible only by being referred to that which is intelligible by itself."[53] Thus human freedom, questioning, and knowing are not intelligible as self-contained activities; but they must be understood in terms of absolute good, truth, and being. Whatever we call the operative principle (final causality, metaphysical causality, principle of intelligibility), the important point is that it is not an extrapolation from particular instances but is known precisely in the original experience of human transcendentality. The formulation of the principle is simply an expression of this deeper unthematic experience. Since this principle cannot be demonstrated in terms of a more comprehensive or generally accepted premise, it can only be defended by a retorsive argument which shows that the act of explicitly denying the principle involves its implicit affirmation.

(d) The vindications do not really arrive at God's existence by bridging the gap between known realities and their ultimate cause. Rather, they claim that God is present from the very beginning as the source of all of our human activities. They make use of a transcendental method which tries to show that the absolute being must be posited as a condition which makes human knowing and willing possible. It is a matter, not of jumping from the finite to the infinite, but of recognizing the abiding presence of the absolute mystery as a necessary condition.

Theistic vindications with these characteristics are designed to avoid many of the standard criticisms of the traditional proofs for God's existence. They do not claim to be strict syllogistic demonstrations; they do not arrive at a being with particular attributes (such as existing up there) which can be refuted by modern science; they do not make a logical deductive jump from the finite world of experience to the existence of an infinite being; they do not employ the disputed principle of efficient causality; they do not begin with concepts and argue to real existence. They do make use of phenomenology, transcendental reduction and deduction, the principle of final causality or intelligibility, and the traditional argument known as "retorsion" in order to vindicate the claim that absolute mystery as gracious source and transcending goal must be present as a condition which makes human experience possible and intelligible.

Most of the refutations of theism in the English-speaking world are still fighting the traditional proofs and have failed to enter into dialogue with the kind of vindication we have presented.[54] There can be no question of claiming an absolutely compelling validity for these vindications (especially considering our brief and sketchy presentation of them), but they do represent a powerful current of thought which has overcome many of the classic objections to theism and which deserves serious consideration today.

IV. AN INDIRECT APPROACH

The abstruse character of these metaphysical arguments makes it important for apologists to work out a simpler, more acceptable defense of their position.

1. As we noted, in defending religious claims an initial argument can be based on an accurate, penetrating phenomenology which convincingly discloses a mystery dimension in experience. It is a matter of presenting it and seeing if it "rings true" or "clicks in." Its truth claim is based on its ability to account for experience in a comprehensive and faithful fashion.

Second, it can be argued that if mystery is obscured, then important areas of experience remain unthematized, to the individual's detriment.[55] Let us imagine an extreme situation where all sense of mystery is lost. Individuals are unaware of the real source of their inner peace and abiding trust and are in constant danger of interpreting them as their own achievement. They have no ultimate basis for respecting the individuality of others. No language is available for properly discussing love and freedom. Death must be repressed because it is unbearable on its own terms. Sin is reduced to neurosis but reappears as a vague, unintelligible disquiet. Human striving is interpreted as contained within the finite, sensible world. The future is seen as that which is ultimately manipulable. There is an attempt to understand persons in terms of functional causes. Various "isms" rush in to fill the void and to play the role of an absolute: materialism, nationalism, scientism, and so on. Questions can be asked, but the ultimate and comprehensive questions about the self and reality are ruled out as nonsense. Life is understood in terms of functional myths and symbols: the sophisticated computer becomes the prime model for self-understanding.

Behavior is understood in terms of programming. Freedom gives way to determinism, love is understood functionally, and truth is reduced to what is empirically verifiable.

Although the situation of an individual or society as a whole never becomes quite as stark as this description (precisely because the mystery can never be totally submerged despite efforts to do so), it seems easy to spot tendencies in this direction today. Where this is the case, human existence is diminished. When significant areas of experience are unexamined and unthematized, our self-understanding is essentially truncated, and the possibilities of effective living are reduced. Persons who repress or deny mystery find themselves in a fundamental living contradiction. Their life performance belies their theory since they are implicitly affirming mystery in practice while theoretically denying it. Their interpretation prevents them from becoming explicitly aware of the deepest sources of their joy and peace as well as the restlessness of their hearts. They are unable to symbolize and celebrate properly the most significant aspects of their lives. In short, persons without a sense of mystery are impoverished.

We could strengthen the two arguments already presented by instituting an explicit comparison between a religious and an irreligious interpretation of life. Which one is more faithful to the full range of human experience, better able to light up the deepest questions of life, and more conducive to effective living? Our contention is that the explicit recognition of mystery is the better option: it gives us a way to interpret and integrate all experience, it encourages us to raise the fundamental questions of life, it accounts for the infinite longings of the heart, it encourages us to break out of the prison of self, it gives us a language for speaking about the kind of experience which evades scientific analysis, it makes us aware of what is already presupposed in our activity, it encourages the celebration of our hopes and dreams, it offers an explanation of our deepest anxiety, it keeps open the possibility of further self-actualization. In brief, the claim is that a recognition of mystery enriches human life.

2. In our indirect approach to justifying a theistic outlook it is important to treat the problems of absurdity and skepticism.

(a) Our phenomenology of human freedom brought to light our longings for a final meaning and a definitive positive outcome to our life. Nothing in this life is able to satisfy these longings. Therefore, unless human striving is absurd, we must posit the absolute good (which we call "God") as its fulfilling goal. The theistic claim, therefore, comes down to an assertion of meaningfulness over absurdity. We can take Sartre as representative of the absurdist position.[56] He argues that man's deepest desire is to escape his contingency and to become the foundation or cause of his own being: in other words, to become what religions call "God." Since this is essentially contradictory, man can never attain it. He is therefore "a useless passion," and life is fundamentally absurd.[57]

The fundamental response to the Sartrian position is that it involves its proponents in a contradictory position. They are claiming absurdity but are implicitly affirming meaning in carrying out their human activities—including arguing for their absurdist position. The contradiction lies between act and verbalization, that is, between the meaningfulness which is implicitly posited in all human activity and the explicit denial of all meaning in life. It might be argued that although the total framework of life is absurd, individual propositions could be meaningful. However, then it would be impossible to account for the particular intelligibility, since such a claim could always be undercut by pointing to the absurdity of the context in which it is uttered.

Furthermore, apologists for theism must try to show that their own interpretation corresponds to our deep-seated longing that our lives ultimately will make sense and to our implicit conviction (manifested in all of our human activity) that they actually do. A case can also be made that the assumption of ultimate meaning is going to be, for most people, a far more powerful motive for constructive human activity than the assumption of ultimate absurdity. Why should individuals develop themselves, meet their responsibilities, serve other people, and contribute to the improvement of the world if good and bad actions are equally pointless? Even if we admit the existence of a few Sisyphian heroes, the vast majority of people cannot function effectively on an absurdist premise.

Once life is interpreted as meaningful rather than absurd, the next step is to show that this is already an implicit acceptance of a limited theism. Human existence interpreted as a closed system is not ultimately meaningful, since human strivings find no final fulfillment. Therefore, if we affirm that life is meaningful, we must posit a gracious transcendent goal which satisfies our longings. Thus, we argue for a limited theistic position by showing the contradiction in an absurdist claim, stressing the human desire for ultimate meaning, and drawing out the theistic implications in an affirmation of meaning.[58]

(b) Our indirect approach must also counter skeptics who claim that the only authentic position on the question of God's existence is an agnostic reserve. We have in mind persons who—because they are aware of complexity, pluralism, and possible objections—think that total commitment to a theistic position is unwarranted.[59]

While admitting that individuals may be unable to make a faith commitment, the apologist for theism must unmask the apparent nobility of the skeptical position in general, which often purports to be the only intellectually honest option and gives the appearance of sophistication. Actually, skepticism in both its theoretical and practical forms is not the detached, neutral outlook that it claims to be. As a theoretical position, it implicitly involves a metaphysical viewpoint (while explicitly denying the possibility of metaphysics) since not to choose is already to take up a position on the great questions. Skepticism is impossible, in practice, since all our human actions presuppose and imply a fundamental outlook on life. Once skepticism is seen as involving an implicit metaphysical view, then it can be brought into dialogue with other world views and be judged on its adequacy and validity as an interpretation of human experience.

Another point to be made in responding to skepticism is that the question of God's existence is not really a speculative question that can be easily set aside as unsolvable. In inquiring about God we are not looking for some strange, powerful being but are asking about the very meaning of our own lives. We are really asking if there is a final fulfillment for our deepest longings, if the source of our existence can be trusted, if the mystery that surrounds us is benign or cruel. In short, the question of God's existence is the question of the meaning or absurdity of our own lives. Viewed in this way, a skeptical reserve is neither desirable nor ultimately possible. We are condemned to take up an attitude toward ourselves.

In addition, it must be shown that life will reveal its richness and potential only to those who are committed. One cannot stand on the sidelines and know the thrill and meaning of the game. Objective talk of love will never capture the reality known by the genuine lover. A mere speculative knowledge leaves many aspects of reality untouched. In the same way, we cannot know the gracious power of the mystery which encompasses us by adopting an attitude of detachment. Mystery reveals itself as trustworthy to those who succeed in surrendering to it.

The whole indirect approach can be seen as an answer to skepticism. It tries to show that belief in the gracious mystery is possible, desirable, and intellectually honest, even though all of the speculative problems are not solved. A man loves his mother and enjoys all the richness of this relationship, even though he has no scientific certitude that this particular woman is his mother.[60] In this example the commitment involved justifies itself; if a man maintained a skeptical reserve on the question, then he would never know the joys, satisfactions, real responsibilities, and such that the committed son knows. Our claim is that commitment to a theistic position functions much the same way. It is an intellectually honest decision based on converging probabilities, and only through such a commitment will a person come to know the graciousness of the mystery of life. It is indeed a circle, but a legitimate and fruitful one.

We have moved within such a circle throughout this book as we identified and worked out the first steps which Christian apologetics must take in order to make an adequate response to the contemporary eclipse of mystery. Thus, we have seen that there are indeed rich and mysterious depths in our interpersonal self-experience which are disclosed by accurate and vivid descriptions of our most fundamental human activities. It was further suggested that this mystery which envelopes and draws us can be characterized as gracious. Finally, I claimed and tried to demonstrate that an intellectually honest vindication of this religious viewpoint is possible. Once this foundation is established, then the apologist is in a position to complete the project by relating the gracious mystery to the God of the Judaeo-Christian tradition and by justifying the claim that Jesus is the definitive revelation of the Mysterious One.

Notes

CHAPTER I: THE ECLIPSE OF MYSTERY

1. The following treatment is dependent on Rahner's ideas. See especially "Problem of Secularization," *TI*, 10, pp. 318–348 (*ST*, 8, pp. 637–666); "Secularization," *TI*, 11, pp. 166–184 (*ST*, 9, pp. 177–196).

2. For an attempt to articulate this ambivalence in terms of secularity and secularism see Shubert Ogden, *Reality of God*, pp. 6–20.

3. "Humanization," *TI*, 14, pp. 300–303 (*ST*, 10, pp. 552–556).

4. For this opinion see Rahner, "Faith and Doctrine," *TI*, 14, p. 35 (*ST*, 10, pp. 273–274).

5. See *The Myth of Sisyphus*.

6. Ontologism is the teaching condemned by the Church which claimed "that human knowledge is made possible only by way of a direct, though non-explicit, vision of the divine essence in itself." See "Ontologism," *Theological Dictionary*, pp. 323–324 (*Theologisches Wörterbuch*, p. 311).

7. *On Death and Dying*.

8. *Whatever Became of Sin?*

9. *An Inquiry into the Human Prospect*.

10. *One-Dimensional Man*.

11. *On Religion*, pp. 11–12.

12. *The Idea of the Holy*, p. 7.

13. *Grace in Freedom*, p. 55 (*Gnade als Freiheit*, p. 83).

CHAPTER II: IN SEARCH OF MYSTERY

1. The word 'mystagogy' has classical origins. Plutarch used it to refer to initiation into the mystery cults. In the fourth century St. Cyril of Jerusalem gave his "Mystagogic Catecheses" which offered further instruction about the rites of sacramental initiation. Rahner, beginning in 1961, has increasingly used the term to describe the need to initiate contemporary people into the true depths of their mysterious existence. While he has never worked out a full explanation or systematic development of this notion (as he himself noted in the Introduction), his scattered references contain valuable suggestions which I am drawing on throughout this book.

2. While Rahner does not use this term, it does reflect his general distinction between categorical (which indicates the objective, reflexive level of human experience) and the transcendental (which often refers to the deeper unthematized aspects of our experience). I am introducing this distinction into the discussion of mystagogy because it allows us to develop the often overlooked fact that there are two distinct apologetic functions. We will treat categorical mystagogy briefly and then develop at great length the meaning and function of a prior apologetic task which we will term 'transcendental mystagogy'.

3. "Future," *TI,* 13, pp. 40–41 (*ST,* 10, pp. 50–51).

4. "Theology and Anthropology," *TI,* 9, p. 29 (*ST,* 8, p. 44).

5. Ibid., p. 42 (*ST,* 8, p. 60).

6. Paul Tillich, *Systematic Theology,* 1, pp. 3–9; ibid., 2, pp. 14–18.

7. Ibid., 2, p. 13.

8. For a criticism of Tillich on this point see Tracy, *Blessed Rage,* p. 46.

9. "The Parish Bookshop," *Market Place,* p. 97 (*Sendung,* p. 478).

10. *Systematic Theology,* 2, p. 15. We should note that this whole section is based on Tillich's explicit theoretical statements on methodology. In actual practice his theology often manifests a more organic approach.

11. "Evangelization," *Crossroads,* p. 41 (*Wagnis,* p. 55).

12. The following is dependent on scattered suggestions by Rahner. For example, see "Secularization," *TI,* 11, pp. 172–175 (*ST,* 9, pp. 183–186).

13. The term 'mystagogue' is introduced here to name those who carry out the mystagogical task of initiating into mystery. The statement that "the apologist must become a mystagogue" is a way of summarizing the thesis of this book. Its meaning can only be developed gradually, but in general it suggests that apologetics must first help people develop a sense of mystery before presenting and defending Christian claims.

14. "Individual Member," *Christian Commitment,* p. 106 (*Sendung,* p. 119).

15. We are reminded of Heidegger's call for more "meditative thinking" in a world dominated by "calculative thinking." For this distinction see Heidegger, *Discourse on Thinking,* pp. 46–57.

16. For those authors who think that the deeper experiences of life such as fundamental trust can be absent or destroyed see Gilkey, *Whirlwind,* p. 354; John Baillie, *The Sense of the Presence of God,* p. 84; Tracy, *Blessed Rage,* p. 187. For a more optimistic view see Ogden, *Reality of God,* pp. 32–43, 114–116.

17. For this formulation see Gilkey, *Whirlwind,* p. 305.

18. For other examples of what we are calling "transcendental mystagogy," done in the context of a larger theological enterprise, see Macquarrie, *Principles,* p. 53–110; Tracy, *Blessed Rage,* pp. 91–118; Gilkey, *Whirlwind,* pp. 315–413; Ogden, *The Reality of God,* pp. 21–43; Lonergan, *Method in Theology,* pp. 101–125; Tillich, *Systematic Theology,* 1, pp. 11–15.

CHAPTER III: THE EXPERIENCE OF MYSTERY

1. "Self and God," *TI,* 13, p. 122 (*ST,* 10, p. 133).

2. For an exploration of the importance of self-actuation in Rahner's

thought see Andrew Tallon, "Rahner and Personization," *Philosophy Today*, 14, 1970, pp. 44–46; Leonardo R. Silos, "A Note on the Notion of 'Selbstvollzug' in Rahner," *Philippine Studies*, 13, 1965, pp. 461–470.

3. For a more ambitious effort to distinguish ten different levels or types of consciousness see Lonergan, *Method in Theology*, pp. 302–305.

4. Rahner's German word 'Katergorical' is variously translated as 'categorial', 'categorical', or 'predicamental' and is often synonymous with a posteriori as opposed to a priori. I prefer to use 'categorical'.

5. For these and other helpful descriptions see Anita Röper, *The Anonymous Christian*, esp. p. 47.

6. "Good Intention," *TI*, 3, p. 106 (*ST*, 3, p. 128).

7. See *SW²*, esp. pp. 277–283 (*GW²*, pp. 200–287). For a helpful development of this point see Vincent P. Branick, *An Ontology of Understanding*, p. 191.

8. For his most extensive treatment see "Symbol," *TI*, 4, pp. 221–252 (*ST*, 4, pp. 275–312).

9. "Self and God," *TI*, 13, p. 115 (*ST*, 10, p. 136).

10. For a helpful explanation of "limit" see Tracy, *Blessed Rage*, esp. pp. 92–118.

11. For the use of this phrase see Karl Jaspers, *Philosophical Faith and Revelation*, pp. 208–210.

12. For an illuminating discussion of "peak-experience" see Maslow, *Religions, Values, and Peak-Experiences*, esp. pp. 59–68.

13. For the development of this idea see Tillich, *Systematic Theology*, 1, pp. 186–201.

14. For the use of this descriptive term see Tracy, *Blessed Rage*, pp. 105–106.

15. For a good instance of this approach see "Pentecost," *Opportunities for Faith*, p. 40 (*Chancen des Glaubens*, pp. 52–53).

16. "Faith," *Encyclopedia*, p. 498.

17. For just a sampling of numerous mystagogical passages, see *TI*, 4, pp. 183–184 (*ST*, 4, pp. 231–232); *TI*, 3, pp. 87–89 (*ST*, 3, pp. 106–108); *TI*, 11, pp. 157–158 (*ST*, 9, pp. 168–169); *TI*, 13, p. 132 (*ST*, 10, p. 144); *Priestly Life*, p. 8–9 (*Einübung priesterlicher Existenz*, p. 20).

18. One is reminded here of the descriptions of "enlightenment experiences" (*satori*) in the Eastern religious traditions. For example, see Aelred Graham, *Zen Catholicism*, pp. 19–21.

19. See Alan Watts, *Psychotheraphy East and West*.

20. For these and similar examples see "God Today," *TI*, 11, pp. 157–158 (*ST*, 9, pp. 168–169).

21. "Teacher," *Theology for Renewal*, p. 104 (*Sendung*, p. 322).

22. For suggestions along this line see Tracy, *Blessed Rage*, pp. 134–136.

23. For a good summary statement by Rahner of this point see "Exerzitienerfahrung," *ST*, 12, p. 174.

24. "Heresy," *TI*, 5, p. 485 (*ST*, 5, pp. 546–547).

25. "Secularization," *TI*, 11, p. 178 ff. (*ST*, 9, p. 190 ff.).

26. For Rahner's own brief, explicit disavowal of Wittgenstein's admonition see "Methodology," *TI*, 11, p. 102 (*ST*, 9, p. 114). For the suggestion of the need to answer Wittgenstein see Fischer, *Der Mensch*, p. 313. For Wittgenstein's admonition see *Tractatus Logico-Philosophicus*, p. 189.

27. For a very helpful development of this theme see Gilkey, *Whirlwind,* p. 305 ff.

28. Our treatment here follows the outline presented in *Foundations,* pp. 51–71 (*Grundkurs,* pp. 61–79).

29. The following is dependent on Rahner's most comprehensive explanation of the notion of "mystery": see "Mystery," *TI,* 4, pp. 36–73 (*ST,* 4, pp. 51–102). For a good summary statement see "Mystery," *Encyclopedia,* pp. 1000–1004.

30. For examples of the fruitful use of the language of "being" see Macquarrie, *Principles,* esp. pp. 104–122; Tillich, *Systematic Theology,* esp. vol. 1, p. 181 ff.

CHAPTER IV: DISCLOSING MYSTERY

1. For this formulation see Tracy, *Blessed Rage,* pp. 8–10.

2. Gilkey, *Whirlwind,* p. 305 ff.

3. For works representative of this trend see Maslow, *Psychology of Being;* Rollo May, *Love and Will;* Viktor Frankl, *Man's Search for Meaning;* Carl Rogers, *On Becoming a Person.*

4. For example, see Thomas Luckmann, *The Invisible Religion;* Berger, *The Sacred Canopy;* Robert Bellah, *Beyond Belief.*

5. See Bleistein, "Mystagogie," pp. 30–43.

6. "Required: A Concrete Political Starting Place," *Continuum,* 6, 1968, pp. 235–236.

7. This is the formulation of Rudolf Otto, who stresses the need for guiding the listener to the point where "the numinous" begins to stir into consciousness. See *The Idea of the Holy,* p. 7. John Macquarrie makes a similar observation in terms of inviting people to enter sympathetically into descriptions of the graciousness of being. He adds the helpful reminder that such interpretative descriptions also need to be tested through comparison, analysis, and so on. See *Principles,* p. 88.

8. For this discovery in relation to the recognition of "peak-experiences" see Maslow, *Religions, Values, and Peak-Experiences,* pp. 84–90.

9. The following is dependent on Rahner's understanding of "primordial words." See "Priest and Poet," *TI,* 3, pp. 294–317 (*ST,* 3, pp. 349–375); "Poetry and the Christian," *TI,* 4, pp. 357–367 (*ST,* 4, pp. 441–454); "Behold This Heart," *TI,* 3, pp. 321–330 (*ST,* 3, pp. 379–390); "The Sacred Heart," *TI,* 3, pp. 331–334 (*ST,* 3, pp. 391–395).

10. For Rahner's use of this term see "Behold This Heart," *TI,* 3, p. 295 (*ST,* 3, p. 350).

11. Rahner's discussion of 'heart' is often linked to an explanation of devotion to the sacred heart of Jesus. The numerous references to this devotion may be explained by the fact that he wrote his unpublished dissertation on the doctrine of the sacred heart in the Fathers. See "Behold This Heart," *TI,* 3, pp. 321–352 (*ST,* 3, pp. 379–415).

12. Macquarrie, *God Talk,* p. 83.

13. Tracy, *Blessed Rage,* p. 133.

14. Gilkey, *Catholicism*, p. 100.

15. For these formulations see Ian Ramsey, *Religious Language*, pp. 11–48.

16. See *Foundations*, pp. 44–51 (*Grundkurs*, pp. 54–61). This material can also be found in *Grace and Freedom*, pp. 183–190 (*Gnade als Freiheit*, pp. 11–18).

17. See Edmund Husserl, *Ideas*, esp. pp. 13–22. For the suggestion of stages of development within the phenomenological movement see Gilkey, *Whirlwind*, p. 278 ff.; Tracy, *Blessed Rage*, p. 47.

18. Gilkey calls this "hermeneutical phenomenology" and distinguishes it from the approach of Paul Ricoeur which investigates symbols. See Gilkey, *Whirlwind*, p. 281.

19. For an example of Ricoeur's approach see *Symbolism of Evil*.

20. For this terminology and the basis for the following explanation of this methodological principle see "Secularization," *TI*, 11, pp. 178–184 (*ST*, pp. 190–196).

21. See "Religiosität," *ST*, 12, p. 594.

22. "Secularization," *TI*, 11, p. 181 (*ST*, 9, p. 193).

23. "God Today," *TI*, 11, p. 155 (*ST*, 9, pp. 166–167); "Nature and Grace," *TI*, 4, p. 185 (*ST*, 4, p. 233).

24. "Modern World," *Christian Commitment*, p. 33 (*Sendung*, p. 42).

25. *Priestly Life*, pp. 7–8 (*Priesterlicher Existenz*, p. 19).

26. For suggestions along this line see "Theology of Christmas," *TI*, 3, pp. 24–28 (*ST*, 3, pp. 35–39).

27. For Rahner's most important treatment of this topic see "Methodology," *TI*, 11, pp. 101–114, esp. p. 111 (*ST*, 9, pp. 113–126, esp. 123–124).

28. "Self and God," *TI*, 13, pp. 131–132 (*ST*, 10, pp. 142–144).

29. For the idea that there are more intense transcendental experiences which seem to thrust themselves into consciousness see "Religiosität," *ST*, 12, pp. 595–596.

CHAPTER V: MYSTAGOGY DEFENDED

1. For an explicit statement of this attitude see Hans Küng, "To Get to the Heart of the Matter II," *Homiletic and Pastoral Review*, 71, July 1971, pp. 28–29.

2. Even Bert van der Heijden, who has written one of the most complete and scholarly commentaries on Rahner's work, states that the experience of grace first becomes the center of attention in *Vision and Prophecies*, originally written in 1948. See van der Heijden, *Darstellung*, p. 201. Klaus Fischer is an important exception to my general statement, especially in his recognition of the influence of Ignatius and the *Spiritual Exercises* on Rahner. See *Der Mensch*, pp. 19–80.

3. Among these early writings we might note: "Le debut d'une doctrine des cinq sens spirituels chez Origene," *Revue d'ascetique et de mystique*, 13, 1932, pp. 113–145; for the German translation, which first appeared in 1975, see "Origenes," *ST*, 12, pp. 111–136; "La doctrine des 'sens spirituels' au Moyen-Age en particulier chez Saint Bonaventure," *Revue d'ascetique et de*

mystique, 14, 1933, pp. 263–299. For a slightly reworked German translation which serves as the basis for the present analysis see "Mittelalter," *ST,* 12, 1975, pp. 137–172; *Encounters with Silence (Worte ins Schweigen,* 1937).

4. For example, see Jacques Maritain, *Degrees of Knowledge,* pp. 122, 130; Eicher, *Wende,* p. 415; Ulrich Browarzik, *Glauben und Denken,* pp. 84–92; Hans Urs von Balthasar, *Cordula oder der Ernstfall,* p. 84; Anthony Kelly, "God: How Near a Relation?" *The Thomist,* 34, 1970, p. 208; Jeremy Moiser, "Why Did the Son of God Become Man?" *The Thomist,* 37, 1973, pp. 301–302.

5. For a good summary statement see *SW²,* p. 406 (*GW²,* p. 405).

6. For Whitehead's similar statement that "The subjectivist principle is that the whole universe consists of elements disclosed in the analysis of the experience of subjects," see *Process and Reality,* p. 193.

7. *Hominisation,* p. 81 (*Hominisation,* p. 70).

8. *Hearers²,* p. 36 (*Hörer²,* p. 54). For further discussion of this point and the reasons for beginning with man see Martin Heidegger, *Being and Time,* pp. 26–35; John Macquarrie, "How Is Theology Possible?" *Union Seminary Quarterly Review,* 18, 1963, p. 296.

9. "Theology and Anthropology," *TI,* 9, p. 28 (*ST,* 8, p. 43).

10. For a summary statement of a similar approach in process thought in terms of the "reformed subjectivist principle" see Ogden, *The Reality of God,* p. 57.

11. This fundamental insight is at the center of all of Rahner's thought. I would summarize its development in this way: it began in an original intuitive sense of the human orientation to mystery, was strengthened by the Ignatian spirituality he learned, found expression in his early interest in the mysticism of Origen and Bonaventure, was philosophically grounded in his metaphysics of knowledge, constituted the guiding principle of his philosophy of religion, and is the powerful center of his theological work.

12. For this interpretation of Rahner see John C. Robertson, "Rahner and Ogden: Man's Knowledge of God," *Harvard Theological Review,* 63, 1970, p. 382.

13. For examples of this approach see Michael Novak, *Ascent of the Mountain;* John Dunne, *The Way of All the Earth;* Sam Keen, *Telling Your Own Story.*

14. For a similar personalistic turn see Lonergan, *Insight,* pp. xvii–xviii; Macquarrie, "How Is Theology Possible?" *Union Seminary Quarterly Review,* 18, 1963, pp. 297–298.

15. *Foreword to Spirit in the World,* pp. xvii–xviii.

16. See *Philosophie der Offenbarung,* 1966.

17. For a summary statement see ibid., p. 172.

18. See *Offenbarung und Transzendenzerfahrung,* 1969.

19. "The Challenge to Protestant Thought," *Continuum,* 6, 1968, p. 243.

20. "Gnade," *Herausforderung des Christen,* p. 131. For one of Rahner's more important statements on this whole topic refer back to his Introduction to this book.

21. "Self and God," *TI,* 13, pp. 127–128 (*ST,* 10, p. 46).

22. "Neighbour and God," *TI,* 6, p. 241 (*ST,* 6, p. 288).

23. This does not appear more clearly in *Spirit in the World* because the context there is a Thomistic metaphysics of knowledge which did not make a point of distinguishing persons and things. For a defense (based on Rahner's notion of "real symbol") of *Hörer des Wortes* against the objection of Simons

and Gerken see T. Mannermaa, "Eine falsche Interpretationstradition von Karl Rahners *Hörer des Wortes?*" *Zeitschrift für katholische Theologie,* 92, 1970, pp. 204–209.

24. This is an impression I have from my personal encounters with him which is reinforced by the following considerations.

25. For an important contribution to this discussion see Peter Mann, "The Transcendental or the Political Kingdom? I & II," *New Blackfriars,* 50, 1969, pp. 805–812, and 51, 1970, pp. 4–16. Mann compares the positions of Rahner and Metz and concludes that they are complimentary rather than contradictory and could fructify each other.

26. For example, see Carl Peter, "The Position of Karl Rahner Regarding the Supernatural: A Comparative Study of Nature and Grace," *Proceedings of the Catholic Theological Society of America,* 20, 1965, pp. 81–94; Thomas J. Motherway, "Supernatural Existential," *Chicago Studies,* 4, 1965, pp. 79–103; Kenneth D. Eberhard, "Karl Rahner and the Supernatural Existential," *Thought,* 46, 1971, pp. 537–561; Regina Bechtle, "Karl Rahner's Supernatural Existential: A Personalist Approach," *Thought,* 48, 1973, pp. 61–77.

27. *Man's Condition,* p. 91.

28. For an example of speaking about a natural experience or knowledge of God divorced from grace see "Theos," *TI,* 1, p. 98 (*ST,* 1, p. 112); "Experience of Grace," *TI,* 3, p. 86 (*ST,* 3, p. 105).

29. See Shepherd, *Man's Condition,* pp. 240–243.

30. Ibid., p. 245.

31. This is the date of his original publication of the article, "Nature and Grace," *TI,* 1, pp. 297–317 (*ST,* 1, pp. 323–346).

32. "Rahner's *Spirit in the World,*" *Journal of Ecumenical Studies,* 7, 1970, pp. 138–144.

33. Ibid., p. 140.

34. For the story of how Rahner's dissertation was not accepted by Martin Honecker because it was not Thomistic enough see Vorgrimler, *Rahner,* pp. 21–25.

35. We should recall that Gilkey was reviewing the second edition which contained Metz's additions.

36. Since the following references are all from *Spirit in the World,* we will simply include the page numbers in the text. The corresponding references to *GW²* are as follows: *SW²,* pp. 57–65 (*GW²,* pp. 71–78), 67–77 (80–90), 117–120 (129–131), 142–145 (153–156), 146–163 (156–172), 169–173 (179–183), 183–187 (192–196), 182 (191), 237 (243), 284–286 (287–290), 387–408 (387–407).

37. For an indication of the value of this contribution see McCool, "The Philosophy of the Human Person in Karl Rahner's Theology," *Theological Studies,* 22, 1961, pp. 537–562.

38. For some positive evaluations of Rahner's philosophical insights see Francis P. Fiorenza, "Karl Rahner and the Kantian Problematic," Introduction to *Spirit in the World,* pp. xix–xxiv; E. L. Mascall, *Openness of Being,* pp. 67–74; J. de Vries, Review of *Geist in Welt, Scholastik,* 15, 1940, pp. 404–409; Joseph Donceel, *The Philosophy of Karl Rahner.*

39. For a summary of various types of Thomistic thought see Helen James John, *The Thomist Spectrum.* For a classic statement of traditional Thomism see Jacques Maritain, *The Degrees of Knowledge.*

40. Maritain, *The Degrees of Knowledge,* p. 263.

41. For this interpretation of Gilson see Bernard Lonergan, "Metaphysics as Horizon," *Collection,* pp. 202–220.

42. For a summary of this movement see Otto Muck, *The Transcendental Method.*

43. For this point and a strong defense of the transcendental method against the neo-Thomists see Donceel, "A Thomistic Misapprehension?" *Thought,* 32, 1957, pp. 189–198.

44. For this argumentation see ibid.

45. "Methodology," *TI,* 11, pp. 84–101 (*ST,* 9, pp. 95–113).

46. For the judgment that Rahner's theology could not survive if his metaphysics of knowledge were to fall before the philosophical attacks of his opponents see McCool, "Philosophy and Christian Wisdom," *Thought,* 44, 1969, pp. 485–512.

47. "Methodology," *TI,* 11, p. 87 (*ST,* 9, p. 98).

48. Ibid.

49. Ibid., p. 89 (pp. 100–101).

50. *Principles,* p. vii.

51. For this point and the following see *Insight,* pp. 348–374.

52. Ibid., p. 350.

53. "An Interview with Fr. Bernard Lonergan," *Second Collection,* p. 229.

54. For a summary statement see *SW²,* p. 383 (*GW²,* pp. 382–383). Here we will simply summarize points which will be treated at length in Chapter Seven.

55. Ibid., p. 391 (pp. 390–391).

56. *The Trinity,* p. 92 (*Mysterium Salutis,* 2, p. 377).

57. *Foundations,* p. 64 (*Grundkurs,* p. 73).

58. "Brief von P. Karl Rahner," in Fischer,*Der Mensch,* 1974, pp. 407–408.

59. For a primary source see William James, *Pragmatism and Other Essays.*

60. Lonergan's discussion is at least suggestive of ways of adding precision to Rahner's broad distinction, even if one is not impressed with his precise numbering or divisions. See *Method in Theology,* pp. 261–281.

61. For a classic example of developing Rahner's ideas in this way see Carlos Cirne-Lima, *Personal Faith.*

62. For some helpful attempts by Westerners to appropriate these traditions see Alan Watts, *Psychotherapy East and West;* Aelred Graham, *The End of Religion.*

63. The work of Ian Ramsey would be especially helpful here. See *Religious Language* and *Models and Mystery.*

64. For this suggestion see Edward MacKinnon, "The Transcendental Turn: Necessary But Not Sufficient," *Continuum,* 6, 1968, pp. 225–231.

65. This was proposed by Paul Ricoeur in his oral response to Rahner's paper on the incomprehensibility of God given at the 1974 septicentennial celebration of Thomas Aquinas at the University of Chicago. For the published version see " 'Response' to Karl Rahner's Lecture: On the Incomprehensibility of God," *The Journal of Religion,* 58, 1978 (Supplement), pp. 126–131. However, I remain far more impressed with the critical function of the analytic tradition in relation to the apologetic task than with its positive constructive possibilities.

CHAPTER VI: MODELS OF MYSTERY EXPLAINED

1. *Whirlwind*, esp. p. 247 ff.
2. Ibid., p. 425.
3. Ibid., p. 454.
4. See *Blessed Rage*, p. 91.
5. *Principles*, pp. 43–173.
6. My project also has particular characteristics in common with a number of other authors: Louis Dupré's descriptions of the fundamental structure of the faith of religious man and his philosophical defense of the fact that man is dialectically related to a transcendent dimension *(The Other Dimension);* Gabriel Moran's exploration of human experience (which is always social and relational) in search of universal revelation *(The Present Revelation);* Peter Berger's attempt to discern what he calls "signals of transcendence" in ordinary experience *(A Rumor of Angels);* Michael Novak's encouragement to examine one's own personal life story as a means of uncovering a sacred or religious dimension *(Ascent of the Mountain);* John Dunne's call for an empathetic passing over to the standpoint of great historical figures as a means of recognizing and expanding one's own religious horizons *(The Way of All the Earth);* Rudolph Otto's use of phenomenology to evoke or awaken a sense of the "numinous" *(The Idea of the Holy);* J. G. Davies' use of "disclosure situations" in order to help his readers recognize the holy in their personal relationships and everyday life *(Every Day God);* Schleiermacher's effort to speak to nonbelievers in order to awaken in them a "sense and taste for the infinite" *(On Religion);* William James' use of a descriptive method and his openness to a wide variety of religious experiences *(The Varieties of Religious Experience);* Sam Keen's attempt to involve his readers in reflections on their own experience in order to discover a deeper dimension *(Telling Your Story);* and finally Henry Duméry's analysis of creative human freedom to reveal the One or the Absolute *(Faith and Reflection)*.
7. *Method in Theology*, pp. 284–285. In adopting this general definition, we are by-passing much of the technical discussion of various types of models. However, it does recall Ian Ramsey's distinction between picture and disclosure models. See *Models and Mystery*, pp. 1–21.
8. Ewert Cousins, "Models and the Future of Theology," *Continuum*, 7, 1969, pp. 78–92.
9. See *Religious Language*, pp. 49–89; *Models and Mystery*.
10. *Religious Language*, p. 64.
11. *Being and Time*, p. 105.
12. Ibid., pp. 105–106, n. 1.
13. For this formulation see Tracy, *Blessed Rage*, p. 215.
14. Ibid., pp. 69–70.
15. For this understanding of the nature of existential truth see Macquarrie, *Principles*, pp. 146–147.
16. "The Task of Philosophical Theology" in *The Future of Philosophical Theology*, ed. Robert Evans, pp. 55–84.
17. See, among other places, "The Response of the Jesuit," *Second Collection*, pp. 170–175.
18. *The Courage To Be*.

19. *On the Eternal in Man,* pp. 35–65.

20. *Whirlwind,* p. 306, n. 1.

21. This term is suggested by Maslow's use of "rhapsodic communication" as a technique for eliciting a recognition of "peak-experiences." See *Religions, Values, and Peak-Experiences,* pp. 84–88.

22. It seems that one of the gains of the younger phenomenologists of religious experience such as Michael Novak, John Dunne, and Gabriel Moran over their masters, Rahner and Lonergan, is precisely the greater appreciation and use of the symbolic and imaginative factor in self-understanding. For an expression of this point see Novak, *Politics: Realism and Imagination,* pp. 9–10.

23. *Systematic Theology,* 1, p. 106.

24. For an explanation of this summary statement of Tillich I am indebted to an unpublished paper by John Macquarrie on the topic of religious experience.

25. *Models and Mystery,* p. 60.

26. For this list see *Whirlwind,* p. 365.

27. *The Courage To Be,* pp. 32–85.

28. *Principles,* pp. 62–68.

29. *Insight.*

30. *Philosophy of God and Theology,* pp. 50–51.

31. *I and Thou.*

32. *Blessed Rage,* pp. 94–109.

33. *Reality of God,* p. 37.

34. *The Way of All the Earth.*

35. *Every Day God,* pp. 129–213.

36. *A Rumor of Angels,* pp. 66–94.

37. *The Present Revelation,* pp. 74–148.

38. *God the Future of Man,* pp. 73–78.

39. *On Being a Christian,* pp. 70–79.

40. *Faith and Reflection,* pp. 143–177.

CHAPTER VII: MODELS OF MYSTERY

1. Lonergan, *Insight,* p. 9.

2. The following analysis of human questioning is dependent on Lonergan, who provides us with an extensive phenomenology of the process of inquiry and learning, which eventually is seen to have being itself as its objective. See *Insight,* esp. pp. 348–359.

3. The following description is dependent on Rahner. See especially *SW*[2], pp. 57–77 (*GW*[2], pp. 71–90); *Hearers*[2], pp. 31 ff. (*Hörer*[2], pp. 43 ff.).

4. Heidegger, *Introduction to Metaphysics,* p. 1.

5. Rahner, "What Is Man?" *Crossroads,* p. 11 (*Wagnis,* p. 13).

6. For an excellent analysis of this phenomenon see Tillich, *Courage To Be,* pp. 32–85.

7. *Hearers*[2], p. 53 (*Hörer*[2], p. 63).

8. For Rahner's development of this point see *SW*[2], p. 57 (*GW*[2], p. 71).

9. The following is based on Rahner's treatment of abstraction. See *SW*², pp. 117–236 (*GW*², pp. 129–242).

10. For this approach and the following explanation, see *Hearers*², pp. 53–68 (*Hörer*², pp. 63–77).

11. Coreth, *Metaphysics,* p. 154.

12. We find Rahner's most complete treatment of this question under the heading *"conversio ad phantasmata."* See *SW*², pp. 237–383 (*GW*², pp. 243–383).

13. The word 'materiality' suggests that we are dealing with a constitutive principle of man and not an original element on the model of physical matter to which is added a soul. See Coreth, *Metaphysics,* p. 157.

14. *Being and Nothingness,* p. 566.

15. For a classic statement of this position see Skinner, *Beyond Freedom and Dignity,* esp. pp. 26–43.

16. The main lines, if not all the details, of the following are dependent on *Foundations,* esp. pp. 26–31, 35–41, and 93–106 (*Grundkurs,* pp. 37–42, 46–53, and 101–112). For a helpful treatment of freedom which develops some of the same themes from a different perspective see Duméry, *Faith and Reflection,* esp. pp. 143–177.

17. For example, Skinner's insight into the influence of environmental factors on behavior ends up viewing the human self as "a repetoire of behavior appropriate to a given set of contingencies." See *Beyond Freedom and Dignity,* p. 199.

18. *Foundations,* p. 29 (*Grundkurs,* p. 40).

19. For a concise explanation of this point see "Freedom," *TI,* 6, pp. 183–186 (*ST,* 6, pp. 221–225).

20. Rahner, *Watch and Pray With Me,* pp. 12–13 (*Heilige Stunde,* pp. 13–14).

21. Rahner, *The Eternal Year,* p. 131 (*Kleines Kirchenjahr,* p. 128).

22. *Theology of Death,* p. 39 (*Zur Theologie des Todes,* p. 30).

23. For the following discussion see "Freedom," *TI,* 6, pp. 179–183 (*ST,* 7, pp. 216–221).

24. For this opinion and the following analysis see "Man of Today," *TI,* 6, pp. 13–15 (*ST,* 6, pp. 25–27).

25. For Sartre's explanation of being condemned to freedom see *Being and Nothingness,* p. 567 ff.

26. For a very helpful analysis of man's sense of impotence despite his growing power to control himself see May, *Love and Will,* p. 185 ff.

27. For the idea that the modern problem of freedom is an inability to achieve wholeheartedness see Robert Johann, "Wholeheartedness," *Building the Human,* pp. 145–147.

28. For a very helpful discussion of the idea that love individuates and personalizes see Teilhard de Chardin, "Sketch of a Personalistic Universe," *Human Energy,* pp. 53–92.

29. For the following analysis see "Ignatian Spirituality," *Market Place,* pp. 141–144 (*Sendung,* pp. 529–531).

30. For a helpful discussion of mutuality upon which the following is dependent see Moran, *The Present Revelation,* pp. 211–216.

31. For Gabriel Marcel's distinction between "problem" and "mystery" and its application to human relationships see *Creative Fidelity,* pp. 147–174.

32. The following discussion is dependent on *Hearers*[2], p. 85 ff. (*Hörer*[2], p. 95 ff.).

33. We should note that freedom could also be established in other ways, especially by beginning in an interpersonal context. For example, see Coreth, *Metaphysics*, pp. 160–169.

34. "The Theology of Freedom," *Grace in Freedom*, p. 216 (*Gnade als Freiheit*, p. 44).

35. Coreth, *Metaphysics*, p. 162.

36. For a very helpful discussion of various modes of thinking and knowing, including the personal, see Macquarrie, *Principles*, pp. 90–96.

37. For the basis of the following see *Foundations*, pp. 26–31 (*Grundkurs*, pp. 37–42).

38. Rahner's early article (1941) on concupiscence remains one of the best sources for this point. See *TI*, 1, pp. 347–382 (*ST*, 1, pp. 377–414).

39. For a discussion of various types of polarities and imbalances in human existence see Macquarrie, *Principles*, pp. 59–74.

40. For systematic treatment of this notion see *Foundations*, pp. 90–115 (*Grundkurs*, pp. 97–121).

41. *Hörer*[1], pp. 125–126.

CHAPTER VIII: MYSTERY VINDICATED

1. The following is dependent on the suggestions of David Tracy. See *Blessed Rage*, pp. 54, 64–92.

2. Ibid., p. 91.

3. Ibid., p. 71.

4. For a warning against this procedure see Ronald Hepburn, *Christianity and Paradox*, pp. 155–185.

5. For a good summary see Gilkey, *Whirlwind*, pp. 3–178. For more recent developments see Tracy, *Blessed Rage*, pp. 146–203.

6. Coreth, *Metaphysics*, pp. 31–32. I am using this broad understanding of transcendental method without going into the diverse forms it takes. For a survey of the various proponents of this method see Otto Muck, *The Transcendental Method*.

7. For example, see John Cobb, *A Christian Natural Theology*.

8. For example, see P. F. Strawson, *Individuals*. For an explanation of how Strawson's "descriptive metaphysics" represents a "distrust of reductionism" see Macquarrie, *God Talk*, p. 113.

9. For a fine collection of essays by various authors (David Burrell, Heinrich Ott, Schubert Ogden, etc.) on this topic see *The Future of Philosophical Theology*, ed. Robert Evans.

10. "Methodology," *TI*, 11, pp. 84–92 (*ST*, 9, pp. 95–100).

11. For a good summary of the objections to the traditional proofs see Macquarrie, *Principles*, pp. 43–54.

12. *On Being a Christian*, pp. 64–88.

13. This is the approach adopted by John Macquarrie which he terms "descriptive and existential" as opposed to "deductive and rationalistic." The

task is to illumine the situation rather than prove by deduction. See *Principles*, pp. 54–58.

14. For this type of argument known as "retorsion" see Donceel, "Can We Still Make a Case in Reason for the Existence of God," *God Knowable and Unknowable*, ed. Robert J. Roth, pp. 170–171.

15. For a summary of Rahner's position on the proofs see *Foundations*, pp. 68–71 (*Grundkurs*, pp. 76–79).

16. Thus the method is called indirect because it strives for certitude while it circumvents particular problems. For his most complete treatment of this method see *Foundations*, pp. 1–14 (*Grundkurs*, pp. 13–25).

17. For the distinction between correspondence, coherence, and pragmatic theories of truth see Eugene Fontinell, *Toward a Reconstruction of Religion*, p. 99 ff.

18. Macquarrie, *Principles*, pp. 147–148.

19. Tillich, *Systematic Theology*, 1, p. 106.

20. Fontinell, *Reconstruction of Religion*, p. 99. Of course, the criteria would have to be specified more precisely in a complete explanation of the pragmatic theory, but here we are simply trying to understand the main lines of an indirect approach.

21. *Critique of Pure Reason*, p. 91.

22. Ibid., p. 487 ff.

23. For this point and the following explanation see Donceel, "God's Existence," pp. 174–177.

24. For an explanation of reduction and deduction see Coreth, *Metaphysics*, p. 37.

25. Most transcendental deductions are based on either judgment or questioning. However, I believe a distinct argument can be made by analyzing abstraction, at least for those who accept the validity of universal concepts.

26. The following is based on SW^2, pp. 143–183 (GW^2, pp. 153–192).

27. I am retaining the Latin term *esse* throughout this analysis because it avoids certain immediate misunderstandings associated with possible translations such as 'being', 'existence', 'Being', 'act of being', etc. For Rahner's understanding of *esse* see ibid., pp. 68–71 (pp. 156–232). For a survey of the meaning of *esse* in the scholastic tradition see Helen James John, *The Thomist Spectrum*.

28. The following is based on the work of Maréchal. See *Maréchal Reader*, ed. Donceel, p. 115 ff.

29. For a helpful explanation of this dynamism which relates Maréchal's ideas to the work of Blondel see Tyrrel, *Man: Believer and Unbeliever*, pp. 169–175.

30. *Maréchal Reader*, p. 145.

31. The following is based on the argument advanced by Coreth. See *Metaphysics*, p. 57 ff.

32. Coreth makes the point that absolute *esse* should not at this stage of the argument be identified with God, which he understands as the ultimate cause transcending all finite beings. This requires further argumentation as we shall see. *Metaphysics*, pp. 65–66.

33. For a very helpful article which places *Spirit in the World* in the framework of the Kantian critique see Fiorenza, Introduction to SW^2, pp. xix–xlv.

34. SW^2, p. 167 (GW^2, p. 177).

35. For this point and the following see ibid., pp. 68–77 (pp. 81–90).

36. Ibid., p. 69 (p. 82). We should note the controversy over Rahner's thesis. O'Donoghue contends that it is illegitimate to jump from the fact that being is knowable to the idea that being is knowing. See "Rahner: Early Philosophy," *Irish Theological Quarterly*, 37, 1970, pp. 322–325. Cornelius Ernst finds this thesis totally unacceptable. See Introduction to *TI*, 1, p. xiii. For a defense of Rahner's position and a refutation of Ernst see Daniel J. Shine, "The Being-Present-To-Itself of Being," *Continuum*, 6, 1968, pp. 240–245. Shubert Ogden thinks that knowing should be seen in relational terms rather than as self-presence. See "The Challenge to Protestant Thought," *Continuum*, 6, 1968, pp. 238–239.

37. For the following see *Foundations*, pp. 66–68 (*Grundkurs*, pp. 75–76).

38. A full explanation would have to root this categorical freedom in a logically prior transcendental freedom in order to set the stage for countering the determinist's denial of free choice.

39. *Metaphysics*, p. 65.

40. The following is a variation of an argument which Joseph Donceel uses to move from the possibility of God's existence to his actual existence. See "God's Existence," pp. 168–169.

41. I hesitate to attribute this position to Rahner without any qualification, but it does represent his practical solution to the problem. See *Foundations*, pp. 51–71 (*Grundkurs*, pp. 61–79).

42. Ibid., p. 69 (p. 77).

43. Ibid., p. 60 (p. 69).

44. For authors who have noted difficulties in Rahner's handling of the relationship between being and God see J. deVries, *Scholastik*, 15, 1940, p. 408; Robert Masson, "Rahner and Heidegger; Being, Hearing, and God," *The Thomist*, 37, 1973, pp. 455–488; Peter Eicher, *Wende*, pp. 163–164; Klaus Fischer, *Der Mensch*, p. 175; Andrew Tallon, "Spirit, Freedom, History," *The Thomist*, 38, 1974, p. 916.

45. *SW²*, pp. 180–181 (*GW²*, p. 190).

46. Ibid., p. 181 (p. 190).

47. *An Ontology of Understanding*, pp. 140–142.

48. David Tracy has suggested that Rahner is to be classed as a neo-orthodox theologian because of his inability to deal with the problem of relationship and change in God. See *Blessed Rage*, p. 30. Joseph Donceel sees more openness in Rahner on this question. See "Second Thoughts on the Nature of God," *Thought*, 46, 1971, pp. 350–353.

49. "Incarnation," *TI*, 4, pp. 113–114, n. 3 (*ST*, 4, p. 147, n. 3).

50. "Panentheism," *Theological Dictionary*, p. 334 (*Theologisches Wörterbuch*, p. 317).

51. Rahner has used the term 'quasi-formal causality' to describe this in order to highlight the fact that this active involvement does not imply imperfection. "Uncreated Grace," *TI*, 1, pp. 330–331 (*ST*, 1, pp. 358–359).

52. I am guided here by Donceel's explanation of his own proof. See "God's Existence," pp. 170–173.

53. Ibid., p. 172.

54. For this assessment, see ibid., p. 159. I personally do not know of any work in English which attempts a detailed refutation of the theistic arguments put forward by men like Rahner, Maréchal, Coreth, and Donceel. In

survey works where one might expect such a dialogue it is not to be found. For example, see John Hick, *Philosophy of Religion*. We should note here the friendly exposition and moderate criticism of transcendental Thomism presented by E. L. Mascall. See *The Openness of Being*. Also of interest is a collection of articles attacking Lonergan from many different angles. See *Looking at Lonergan's Method*, ed. Patrick Corcoran.

55. This is the fundamental argument used by Gilkey in his prolegomenon to theology. See *Whirlwind*, p. 305.

56. We could also recall Camus' understanding of Sisyphus as the absurd hero. See *The Myth of Sisyphus*. We should at least note that Duméry distinguishes Sartre's position from the absurdists. See *Faith and Reflection*, pp. 19–20. However, for our purpose it seems legitimate to link them.

57. *Being and Nothingness*, p. 784. We must grant that Sartre sounds more realistic, more in touch with the dark side of life, more convincing in his description, than many apologists for theism.

58. For this argument see Donceel, "God's Existence," pp. 180–182.

59. For Rahner's treatment of skepticism upon which the following is based see "Intellectual Honesty," *TI*, 7, pp. 48–58 (*ST*, 7, pp. 55–64).

60. Rahner often employs this example against skepticism. See ibid., p. 54 (p. 60).

Bibliography

I. WORKS BY KARL RAHNER

A. Books

Allow Yourself to Be Forgiven: Penance Today. Trans. by Salvator Attanasio. Denville, N.J.: Dimension Books, 1975. (*Man darf sich vergeben lassen.* Munich: Ars Sacra, 1974.)

Belief Today. Trans. by M. H. Heelan, Ray and Rosaleen Ockendon, and William Whitman with a Preface by Hans Küng. New York: Sheed and Ward, 1967. (Combines: *Alltägliche Dinge.* Einsiedeln: Benziger, 1964; *Im Heute glauben.* Einsiedeln: Benziger, 1965; "Intellectuelle Redlichkeit und christlicher Glaube." *Stimmen der Zeit,* 177, 1966, pp. 401–417).

Biblical Homilies. Trans. by Desmond Forristal and Richard Strachan. New York: Herder and Herder, 1966. (*Biblische Predigten.* Freiburg: Herder, 1965.)

Bishops: Their Status and Function. Trans. by Edward Quinn. London: Burns & Oates, 1964 ("Über der Episkopat," *Das Amt der Einheit.* Ed. by W. Stahlin et al. Stuttgart: Schwaberverlag, 1964.)

With Haussling, Angelus. *The Celebration of the Eucharist.* Trans. by W. J. O'Hara. New York: Herder and Herder, 1968. (*Die vielen Messen und das eine Opfer.* Freiburg: Herder, 1966.)

Christian at the Crossroads. Trans by V. Green. London: Burns & Oates, 1975; Abbr. *Crossroads.* (This translation contains 14 of the 21 articles in *Wagnis des Christen: Geistliche Texte.* Freiburg: Herder, 1974; Abbr. *Wagnis.*)

The Christian Commitment: Essays in Pastoral Theology. Trans. by Cecily Hastings. New York: Sheed and Ward, 1963. (Part 1 of *Sendung und Gnade.*) In England: *Mission and Grace.* Vol. 1. London: Sheed and Ward, 1963.

Christian in the Market Place. Trans. by Cecily Hastings. New York: Sheed and Ward, 1966; Abbr. *Market Place.* (Part 3 of *Sendung und Gnade.*) In England: *Mission and Grace.* Vol. 3. London: Sheed and Ward, 1966.

The Church after the Council. Trans. by Davis C. Herron and Rodelinde Albrecht. New York: Herder and Herder, 1966. (Includes: *Das Konzil— ein neuer Beginn.* Freiburg: Herder, 1966; "Das neue Bild der Kirche," *Geist und Leben,* 39, 1966; *Die Herausforderung der Theologie durch das II. Vatikanische Konzil.* Freiburg: Herder, 1966.)

Ed. *Concilium: Theology in the Age of Renewal* (Pastoral Theology). New York: Paulist Press, 1965–1969.

Ed. *The Pastoral Mission of the Church.* Vol. 3. 1965.

Ed. *Re-thinking the Church's Mission.* Vol. 13. 1966.

Ed. *The Pastoral Approach to Atheism.* Vol. 23. 1967.

Ed. *The Renewal of Preaching.* Vol. 33. 1968.

Do You Believe in God? Trans. by Richard Strachan. New York: Paulist Press, 1969. (*Glaubst du an Gott?* Munich: Ars Sacra, 1967.)

Encounters with Silence. Trans. by James M. Demske. Westminster, Md.: Newman Press, 1960. (*Worte ins Schweigen.* Innsbruck: Felizian Rauch, 1938.)

Ed. *Encyclopedia of Theology: The Concise Sacramentum Mundi.* Trans. by John Griffiths, Francis McDonagh, and David Smith. New York: Seabury, 1975; Abbr. *Encyclopedia.* Rahner himself contributed 85 of the articles.

The Eternal Year. Trans. by John Shea. Baltimore: Helicon Press, 1964. (*Kleines Kirchenjahr.* Munich: Ars Sacra, 1954.)

Everyday Faith. Trans. by W. J. O'Hara. New York: Herder and Herder, 1968. (*Glaube, der die Erde liebt.* Freiburg: Herder, 1966; Abbr. *Glaube.*).

Faith Today. Trans. by Ray and Rosaleen Ockendon. London: Sheed and Ward, 1967. (*Im Heute glauben.* Einsiedeln: Benziger, 1965.)

Foundations of Christian Faith: An Introduction to the Idea of Christianity. Trans. by William V. Dych. New York: Seabury, 1978; Abbr. *Foundations.* (*Grundkurs des Glaubens: Einführung in den Begriff des Christentums.* Freiburg: Herder, 1976; Abbr. *Grundkurs.*)

Freiheit und Manipulation in Gesellschaft und Kirche. 2nd ed. München: Kösel, 1971.

Das freie Wort in der Kirche. Einsiedeln: Johannes, 1953.

Grace in Freedom. Trans. by Hilda Graef. New York: Herder and Herder, 1969. (*Gnade als Freiheit: Kleine theologische Beiträge.* Freiburg: Herder, 1968.)

With Arnold, F. X.; Schurr, V.; and Klostermann, F.; eds. *Handbuch der Pastoraltheologie.* Vol. 1–4. Freiburg: Herder, 1964–1969; Abbr. *HPTh.*

Hearers of the Word. Trans. by Michael Richards with a Preface by J. B. Metz. New York: Herder and Herder, 1969; Abbr. *Hearers²*. (*Hörer des*

Wortes: Zur Grundlegung einer Religionsphilosophie. 2nd ed. revised by J. B. Metz. Freiburg: Herderbücherei, 1971; Abbr. *Hörer²*.)

Herausforderung des Christen: Meditationen—Reflexionen. Freiburg: Herderbücherei, 1975.

Hörer des Wortes: Zur Grundlegung einer Religionsphilosophie. 1st ed. Munchen: Kösel-Pustet, 1941; Abbr. *Hörer¹*. Joseph Donceel has prepared a complete translation of this first edition which I have used. Portions of this otherwise unpublished translation appear in *A Rahner Reader.* Ed. by Gerald A. McCool. New York: Seabury, 1975, pp. 2–65.

Inquiries: Inspiration in the Bible; Visions and Prophecies; The Church and the Sacraments; The Episcopate and the Primacy; On Heresy. New York: Herder and Herder, 1964. This is a collection of 5 monographs from the *Quaestiones Disputatae* Series. In England: *Studies in Modern Theology.* London: Burns & Oates, 1965.

With Lehmann, Karl. *Kerygma and Dogma.* Trans. by William Glen-Doepel and ed. by Thomas F. O'Meara. New York: Herder and Herder, 1969. (A section from: *Mysterium Salutis.* Vol. 1. Ed. by Johannes Feiner and Magnus Löhrer. Einsiedeln: Benziger, 1965, pp. 622–703).

Kritisches Wort: Aktuelle Probleme in Kirche und Welt. Introductions by Roman Bleistein. Freiburg: Herderbücherei, 1970.

Leading a Christian Life. Trans. by S. Attanasio, D. White, and J. Quigles. Denville, N.J.: Dimension Books, 1970. (Comprised of 6 short works originally published by Ars Sacra in Munich: *Ewiges Ja,* 1958; *Glaubend und Liebend,* 1957; *Die Gnade wird es vollenden,* 1957; *Das Geheimnis unseres Christus,* 1959; *Bergend und heilend,* 1965.)

With Höfer, Joseph, eds. *Lexicon für Theologie und Kirche.* 2nd ed. Vols. 1–10. Freiburg: Herder, 1957–1967.

Mary, Mother of the Lord. Trans. by W. J. O'Hara. Glasgow: The University Press, 1963. (*Maria, Mutter des Herrn.* Freiburg: Herder, 1956.)

Meditations on Hope and Love. Trans. by V. Green. London: Burns & Oates, 1976. (*Was sollen wir jetzt tun?* and *Gott ist Mensch geworden.* Freiburg: Herder, 1974–1975.)

Meditations on Priestly Life. Trans. by Edward Quinn. London: Sheed and Ward, 1973; Abbr. *Priestly Life.* (*Einübung priesterlicher Existenz.* Freiburg: Herder, 1970.) In the U.S.A.: *The Priesthood.* New York: Seabury, 1973.

Nature and Grace: Dilemmas in the Modern Church. Trans. by Dinah Wharton. New York: Sheed and Ward, 1964. (Chapters 1, 2, 3, and 5 are found in: *Gefahren im heutigen Katholizismus.* Einsiedeln: Johannes, 1950.)

A New Baptism in the Spirit: Confirmation Today. Trans. by Salvator Attanasio. Denville, N.J.: Dimension Books, 1975. (*Auch heute weht der Geist.* Munich: Ars Sacra, 1974.)

On Prayer. New York: Paulist Deus Book, 1968. (*Von der Not und dem Segen des Gebetes.* 6th ed. Freiburg: Herderbücherei, 1964; Abbr. *Gebetes.*) In Ireland: *Happiness through Prayer.* Dublin: Clonmore and Reynolds, 1958.

Opportunities for Faith: Elements of a Modern Spirituality. Trans. by Edward Quinn. New York: Seabury, 1974. (*Chancen des Glaubens: Fragmente einer modernen Spiritualität.* Freiburg: Herderbücherei, 1971.)

With Schlier, Heinrich, eds. *Quaestiones Disputatate.* New York: Herder and Herder, 1961–1967. This series is published first in Freiburg by Herder. The volume numbers in the German and English series sometimes differ and in this listing appear immediately after the title with the abbreviation Q.D.

Inspiration in the Bible. Q.D. 1. Trans. by Charles Henkey. 1961. (*Über die Schriftinspiration.* Q.D. 1. 1957.)

On the Theology of Death. Q.D. 2. Trans. by Charles Henkey. 1961. (*Zur Theologie des Todes.* Q.D. 2. 1958.)

With Ratzinger, Joseph. *The Episcopate and the Primacy.* Q.D. 4. Trans. by Kenneth Barker et al. 1962. (*Episkopat und Primat.* Q.D. 11. 1961.)

Church and the Sacraments. Q.D. 9. Trans. by W. J. O'Hara. 1963. (*Kirche und Sakramente.* Q.D. 10. 1961.)

Visions and Prophecies. Q.D. 10. Trans. by Charles Henkey and Richard Strachan. 1963. (*Visionen und Prophezeiungen.* Q.D. 4. 1958.)

On Heresy. Q.D. 11. Trans. by W. J. O'Hara. 1964. ("Was ist Häresie?" *Häresien der Zeit.* Ed. by A. Böhm. Freiburg: Herder, 1961, pp. 9–44.)

Dynamic Element in the Church. Q.D. 12. Trans. by W. J. O'Hara. 1964. (*Das Dynamische in der Kirche.* Q.D. 5. 1958.)

Hominisation: The Evolutionary Origin of Man as a Theological Problem. Q.D. 13. Trans by W. J. O'Hara, 1965. ("Die Hominisation als theologische Frage." *Das Problen der Hominisation,* by K. Rahner and P. Overhage. Freiburg: Herder, 1961; Abbr. *Hominisation.*)

With Ratzinger, Joseph. *Revelation and Tradition.* Q.D. 17. Trans. by W. J. O'Hara. 1966. (*Offenbarung und Überlieferung.* Q.D. 25. 1965.)

The Christian of the Future. Q.D. 18. Trans. by W. J. O'Hara. 1967. (This is a collection of 4 articles from *Schriften zur Theologie* 6: "Kirche im Wandel," "Zur 'Situationsethik' aus ökumenischer Sicht," "Grenzen der Amtskirche," and "Konziliare Lehre der Kirche und kunftige Wirklichkeit christlichen Lebens.")

With Thüsing, Wilhelm. *Christologie: systematische und exegetisch.* Q.D. 55. 1972.

Vorfragen zu einem ökumenischen Amtsverständnis. Q.D. 65. 1974.

The Religious Life Today. Trans. by V. Green. London: Burns & Oates, 1976. (7 of the 10 articles are from *Wagnis des Christen: Geistliche Texte.* Freiburg: Herder, 1974.)

Et al, eds. *Sacramentum Mundi: An Encyclopedia of Theology.* Vols. 1–6. Trans. by W. J. O'Hara et al. New York: Herder and Herder, 1968–1970.

Schriften zur Theologie. Vols. 1–12. Einsiedeln: Benziger, 1954–1975; Abbr. *ST.* Two volumes are not yet completely translated into English: *Frühe Bussgeschichte.* Vol. 11. 1973. *Theologie aus Erfahrung des Geistes.* Vol. 12. 1975.

Sendung und Gnade: Beiträge zur Pastoraltheologie. 3rd ed. Innsbruck: Tyrolia, 1961; Abbr. *Sendung.*

Servants of the Lord. Trans. by Richard Strachan. New York: Herder and Herder, 1968 (*Knechte Christi: Meditationen zum Priestertum.* Freiburg: Herder, 1967.)

The Shape of the Church to Come. Trans. and with an Introduction by Edward Quinn. New York: The Seabury Press, 1974. (*Strukturwandel der Kirche als Aufgabe und Chance.* Freiburg: Herderbücherei, 1972.)

Spirit in the World. Trans. by William Dych with a Foreword by Johannes B. Metz and an Introduction by Francis P. Fiorenza. New York: Herder and Herder, 1968; Abbr. *SW²*. (*Geist in Welt: zur Metaphysik der endlichen Erkenntnis bei Thomas von Aquin.* 2nd ed. revised by J. B. Metz. München: Kösel, 1957. Abbr. *GW²*.) The original *Geist in Welt* was published at Innsbruck by F. Rauch in 1939. I have used the abbreviation *SW²* for *Spirit in the World* to make clear that it is a translation of the 2nd German edition.

Spiritual Exercises. Trans. by Kenneth Baker. London: Sheed and Ward, 1967. (*Betrachtungen zum ignatianischen Exerzitienbuch.* Munich: Kösel, 1965.)

Ed. *The Teaching of the Catholic Church: As Contained in Her Documents.* Trans. by Geoffrey Stevens. Originally prepared by Joseph Neuner and Heinrich Roos. Staten Island, N.Y.: Alba House, 1967. (*Der Glaube der Kirche in den Urkunden der Lehrverkündigung.* 7th ed. Regensburg: Pustet, 1965.)

With Vorgrimler, Herbert. *Theological Dictionary.* Ed. by Cornelius Ernst and trans. by Richard Strachan. New York: Herder and Herder, 1965. (*Kleines Theologisches Wörterbuch.* Freiburg: Herderbucherei, 1961.) I used the fully revised 10th edition published in 1976 by Herder in Freiburg.

Theological Investigations. Vols. 1–16. Vols. 1–6 published in Baltimore by Helicon; Vols. 7–10 in New York by Herder and Herder; and Vols. 11–14 in New York by Seabury; 1961–1976; Abbr. *TI.* (*Schriften zur Theologie.* Vol. 1–12. Einsiedeln: Benziger, 1954–1975. Abbr. *ST.*) Note that Vol. 15 has not yet appeared in English.

God, Christ, Mary and Grace. Vol. 1. Trans. with an Introduction by Cornelius Ernst. 1961. (*Gott, Christus, Maria, Gnade.* Vol. 1. 1954.)

Man in the Church. Vol. 2. Trans. by Karl H. Kruger. 1963. (*Kirche und Mensch.* Vol. 2. 1955.)

The Theology of the Spiritual Life. Vol. 3. Trans. by Karl H. Kruger and Boniface Kruger. 1967. (*Zur Theologie des Geistlichen Lebens.* Vol. 3. 1956.)

More Recent Writings. Vol. 4. Trans. by Kevin Smyth. 1966. (*Neuere Schriften.* Vol. 4. 1960.)

Later Writings. Vol. 5. Trans. by Karl H. Kruger. 1966. (*Neuere Schriften.* Vol. 5. 1962.)

Concerning Vatican Council II. Vol. 6. Trans. by Karl H. Kruger and Boniface Kruger. 1969. (*Neuere Schriften.* Vol. 6. 1965.) Five articles are missing in the English translation, four of which appear in *The Christian of the Future.*

Further Theology of the Spiritual Life 1. Vol. 7. Trans. by David Bourke. 1971. (First part of: *Ein Grundriss des Geistlichen Lebens.* Vol. 7. 1967.)

Further Theology of the Spiritual Life. 2. Vol. 8. Trans. by David Bourke. 1971. (Second part of: *ST* 7.)

Writings of 1965–1967 1. Vol. 9. Trans. by Graham Harrison. 1972. (First part of: *Theologische Vorträge und Abhandlungen.* Vol. 8. 1967.)

Writings of 1965–1967 2. Vol. 10. Trans. by David Bourke. 1974. (Second part of: *ST* 8.)

Confrontations 1. Vol. 11. Trans. by David Bourke. 1974. (First part of *Konfrontationen.* Vol. 9. 1970.)

Confrontations 2. Vol. 12. Trans. by David Bourke. 1974. (Second part of: *ST* 9.)

Theology, Anthropology, Christology. Vol. 13. Trans. by David Bourke. 1975. (First part of: *Im Gespräch mit der Zukunft.* Vol. 10. 1972.)

Ecclesiology, Questions in the Church, The Church in the World. Vol. 14. Trans. by David Bourke. 1976. (Second part of *ST* 10.)

Experience of the Spirit: Source of Theology. Vol. 16. Trans. by David Moreland. 1979. (First part of: *Theologie aus Erfahrung des Geistes.* Vol. 12. 1975.)

Theology for Renewal: Bishops, Priests, Laity. Trans. by Cecily Hastings and Richard Strachan. New York: Sheed and Ward, 1964. (Part 2 of *Sendung und Gnade.*) In England: *Mission and Grace.* Vol. 2. London: Sheed and Ward, 1964.

Theology of Pastoral Action. Trans. by W. J. O'Hara with adaptations by Daniel Morrissey. New York: Herder and Herder, 1968. ("Grundlegung der

Pastoraltheologie als praktische Theologie." *Handbuch der Pastoraltheologie.* Vol. 1. Freiburg: Herder, 1964, pp. 117–215; Abbr. *HPTh.*)

The Trinity. Trans. by Joseph Donceel. London: Burns & Oates, 1970. ("Der dreifaltige Gott als transzendenter Urgrund der Heilsgeschichte," *Mysterium Salutis.* Vol. 2. Ed. by Johannes Feiner and Magnus Löhrer. Einsiedeln: Benziger, 1967, pp. 317–401.)

Watch and Pray with Me. Trans. by William V. Dych. London: Burns & Oates, 1968. (*Heilige Stunde und Passionsandacht.* Freiburg: Herder, 1955.)

Zur Theologie der Zukunft. Munchen: Deutscher Taschenbuch, 1971. This is a collection of articles from *Schriften* 4, 5, 6, 8, and 9 which concern the theme of the "future."

B. Articles

"A Critique of Hans Küng." *Homiletic and Pastoral Review* 71, May 1971:18–26.

"Reply to Hans Küng." *Homiletic and Pastoral Review* 71, August–September 1971:11–31.

"Letter to Hans Küng from Karl Rahner." *America* 129, July 1973:11–12.

"Die Gotteserfahrung heute." *Zeitschrift für Wissenschaft, Kunst und Literatur* 31, 1975:1261–1266.

"The Faith of the Priest Today." *Philippine Studies* 13, 1965:495–503. ("Der Glaube des Priesters heute." *Orientierung* 26, 1962:215–219, 227–231.)

"The Concept of Existential Philosophy in Heidegger." Trans. by Andrew Tallon. *Philosophy Today* 13, 1969:126–137. ("Introduction au concept de philosophie existentiale chez Heidegger." *Recherches de sciences religieuses* 30, 1940:152–171.)

"Christ as the Exemplar of Clerical Obedience." In *Obedience and the Church.* Trans. by Geoffrey Chapman. Washington: Corpus Books, 1968, pp. 1–18.

C. Unpublished Manuscripts

These materials are available in the library of the Philosophische Hochschule Berkmanskolleg Pullach in Munich.

"Errores Principales in Materia Gratiae." 1947.

"De Deo Creante et Elevante et De Peccato Originali." 1953.

"Mariologie." Innsbruch, 1959.

"De Gratia Christi." 1937–1938.

"De Poenitentia: Tractatus Historico-Dogmaticus." 2nd ed. 1952. The first part of this material appears in *Schriften,* vol. 11.

II. WORKS BY OTHER AUTHORS

A. Books

Baillie, John. *Our Knowledge of God.* London: Humphrey Milford, 1939.

―――. *The Sense of the Presence of God.* London: Oxford University Press, 1963.

Balthasar, Hans Urs von. *Cordula oder der Ernstfall.* 2nd ed. Einsiedeln: Johannes, 1967.

Bellah, Robert. *Beyond Belief.* New York: Harper and Row, 1970.

Bent, Charles N. *Interpretating the Doctrine of God.* New York: Paulist Press, 1969.

Berger, Peter L. *A Rumor of Angels: Modern Society and the Rediscovery of the Supernatural.* New York: Doubleday, 1969.

―――. *The Sacred Canopy.* Garden City, N.Y.: Doubleday, 1969.

Bleistein, Roman, and Klinger, Elmar, eds. *Bibliographie Karl Rahner 1924–1969.* Freiburg: Herder, 1969.

―――. *Bibliographie Karl Rahner 1969–1974.* Freiburg: Herder, 1974.

Branick, Vincent P. *An Ontology of Understanding: Karl Rahner's Metaphysics of Knowledge in the Context of Modern German Hermeneutics.* St. Louis: Marianist Communication Center, 1974.

Browarzik, Ulrich. *Glauben und Denken: Dogmatische Forschung zwischen der Tranzendentaltheologie Karl Rahners und der Offenbarungstheologie Karl Barths.* Berlin: deGruyter, 1970.

Buber, Martin. *I and Thou.* 2nd ed. Trans. by Ronald Gregor Smith. New York: Scribner's, 1958.

Burke, Ronald. "Rahner and Revelation." Ph.D. dissertation, Yale University, 1974.

Camus, Albert. *The Myth of Sisyphus and Other Essays.* Trans. by Justin O'Brien. New York: Vintage Books, 1955.

Cirne-Lima, Carlos. *Personal Faith: A Metaphysical Inquiry.* Trans. by G. Richard Dimler. New York: Herder and Herder, 1965.

Cobb, John B. *A Christian Natural Theology: Based on the Thought of Alfred North Whitehead.* Philadelphia: Westminster Press, 1965.

Corcoran, Patrick, ed. *Looking at Lonergan's Method.* Dublin: The Talbot Press, 1975.

Coreth, Emerich. *Metaphysics.* English edition by Joseph Donceel with a critique by Bernard J. F. Lonergan. New York: Seabury, 1973.

Cousins, Ewert, ed. *Process Theology: Basic Writings.* New York: Newman Press, 1971.

Davies, J. G. *Every Day God: Encountering the Holy in World and Worship.* London: SCM Press, 1973.

Donceel, Joseph. *The Philosophy of Karl Rahner.* New York: Magi Books, 1969.

Duméry, Henry. *Faith and Reflection.* Ed. and with an Introduction by Louis Dupré. Trans. by Stephen McNierney and Mother M. Benedict Murphy. New York: Herder and Herder, 1968.

Dunne, John. *The Way of All the Earth.* 1972. Reprint. Notre Dame: University of Notre Dame Press, 1978.

Dupré, Louis. *The Other Dimension: A Search for the Meaning of Religious Attitudes.* New York: Doubleday, 1972.

Eicher, Peter. *Die anthropologische Wende: Karl Rahners philosophischer Weg vom Wesen des Menschen zur personalen Existenz.* Freiburg, Schweiz: Universitätsverlag, 1970; Abbr. *Wende.*

Evans, Robert, ed. *The Future of Philosophical Theology.* Philadelphia: Westminster Press, 1971.

Fischer, Klaus P. *Der Mensch als Geheimnis: Die Anthropologie Karl Rahners.* Mit einem Brief von Karl Rahner. Freiburg: Herder, 1974; Abbr. *Der Mensch.*

Fontinell, Eugene. *Toward a Reconstruction of Religion: A Philosophical Probe.* Garden City, N.Y.: Doubleday, 1970.

Frankl, Viktor. *Man's Search for Meaning.* Boston: Beacon Press, 1959.

Gelpi, Donald L. *Life and Light: A Guide to the Theology of Karl Rahner.* New York: Sheed and Ward, 1966.

Gerkin, Alexander. *Offenbarung und Transzendenzerfahrung: Kritische Thesen zu einer künftigen dialogischen Theologie.* Dusseldorf: Patmos, 1969.

Gilkey, Langdon. *Catholicism Confronts Modernity: A Protestant View.* New York: Seabury, 1975; Abbr. *Catholicism.*

————. *Naming the Whirlwind: The Renewal of God-Language.* New York: Bobbs-Merrill, 1969; Abbr. *Whirlwind.*

Graham, Aelred. *The End of Religion.* New York: Harcourt Brace Jovanovich, 1971.

————. *Zen Catholicism.* New York: Harcourt Brace and World, 1963.

Heidegger, Martin. *Being and Time.* Trans. by John Macquarrie and Edward Robinson. New York: Harper and Row, 1962.

————. *Discourse on Thinking.* Trans. by John M. Anderson and E. Hans Freund with an Introduction by John M. Anderson. New York: Harper and Row, 1966.

————. *An Introduction to Metaphysics.* Trans. by Ralph Manheim. Garden City, N.Y.: Doubleday Anchor Books, 1961.

Heilbroner, Robert L. *An Inquiry into the Human Prospect.* New York: W.W. Norton and Company, Inc., 1974.

Hepburn, Ronald. *Christianity and Paradox.* London: Watts, 1958.

Hick, John H. *Philosophy of Religion.* 2nd ed. Englewood Cliffs: Prentice-Hall, 1973.

Hoeres, W. *Kritik der transzendentalphilosophischen Erkenntnistheorie.* Stuttgart: Kohlhammer, 1969.

Husserl, Edmund. *Ideas: General Introduction to Pure Phenomenology.* Trans. by W. R. Boyce Gibson. New York: Macmillan, 1931.

James, William. *Pragmatism and Other Essays.* New York: Washington Square Press, 1963.

————. *The Varieties of Religious Experience: A Study in Human Nature.* Introduction by Reinhold Niebuhr. New York: Collier Books, 1961.

Jaspers, Karl. *Philosophical Faith and Revelation.* Trans. by E. B. Ashton. New York: Harper and Row, 1967.

Johann, Robert. *Building the Human.* New York: Herder and Herder, 1968.

John, Helen James. *The Thomist Spectrum.* New York: Fordham University Press, 1966.

Kant, Immanuel. *Critique of Pure Reason.* Unabridged ed. Trans. by Norman Kemp Smith. New York: St. Martin's Press, 1965.

Keen, Sam, and Fox, Anne Valley. *Telling Your Story.* Garden City, N.Y.: Doubleday, 1973.

Kübler-Ross, Elisabeth. *On Death and Dying.* New York: Macmillan, 1969.

Küng, Hans. *On Being a Christian.* Trans. by Edward Quinn. Garden City, N.Y.: Doubleday, 1974.

Lonergan, Bernard. *Collection.* Ed. by F. E. Crowe. New York: Herder and Herder, 1967.

————. *Insight: A Study of Human Understanding.* 3rd ed. New York: Philosophical Library, 1970.

————. *Method in Theology.* New York: Herder and Herder, 1972; Abbr. *Method.*

————. *A Second Collection.* Ed. by William Ryan and Bernard Tyrrell. Philadelphia: The Westminster Press, 1974.

Luckmann, Thomas. *The Invisible Religion: The Problem of Religion in Modern Society.* New York: Macmillan, 1966.

Macquarrie, John. *God-Talk: An Examination of the Language and Logic of Theology.* London: SCM Press, 1967.

————. *Principles of Christian Theology.* 2nd ed. New York: Scribner's, 1977; Abbr. *Principles.*

Marcel, Gabriel. *Creative Fidelity*. Trans. with an Introduction by Robert Rosthall. New York: Noonday Press, 1964.

Marcuse, Herbert. *One Dimensional Man: Studies in the Ideology of Advanced Industrial Society*. Boston: Beacon Press, 1964.

Maréchal, Joseph. *A Maréchal Reader*. Ed. and trans. by Joseph Donceel. New York: Herder and Herder, 1970.

Maritain, Jacques. *The Degrees of Knowledge*. Trans. by Bernard Wall and Margot R. Adamson. London: The Centenary Press, 1937.

Mascall, E. L. *The Openness of Being: Natural Theology Today*. London: Darton, Longman and Todd, 1971.

Maslow, Abraham. *Religions, Values and Peak-Experiences*. New York: Viking Press, 1970.

———. *Toward a Psychology of Being*. 2nd ed. Princeton, N.J.: D. Van Nostrand, 1968; Abbr. *Psychology of Being*.

May, Rollo. *Love and Will*. New York: W. W. Norton, 1969.

McCool, Gerald A., ed. *A Rahner Reader*. New York: Seabury, 1975.

———. *The Theology of Karl Rahner*. Albany: Magi Books, 1969.

McShane, Philip, ed. *Language Truth and Meaning: Papers from the International Lonergan Congress 1970*. Notre Dame: University of Notre Dame Press, 1972.

Menninger, Karl. *Whatever Became of Sin?* New York: Hawthorn Books, 1973.

Metz, Johannes Baptist. *Christliche Anthropozentrik: Über die Denkform des Thomas von Aquin*. Mit einem einführenden Essay von K. Rahner. München: Kösel, 1962.

——— et al. *Gott in Welt: Festgabe für Karl Rahner,* 2 vols. Freiburg: Herder, 1964.

———. *Faith in History and Society: Toward a Practical Fundamental Theology*. Trans. by David Smith. New York: Seabury, 1979.

Moran, Gabriel. *The Present Revelation: In Quest of Religious Foundations*. New York: Herder and Herder, 1972.

Muck, Otto. *The Transcendental Method*. Trans. by William D. Seidensticker. New York: Herder and Herder, 1968.

Neufeld, Karl N., and Bleistein, Roman. *Rahner—Register: Ein Schlüssel zu Karl Rahners 'Schriften zur Theologie I–X' und zu Seinen Lexikonartikeln*. Einleitung von Roman Bleistein. Zurich: Benziger, 1974.

Novak, Michael. *Ascent of the Mountain, Flight of the Dove*. New York: Harper and Row, 1971.

———. *Politics: Realism and Imagination*. New York: Herder and Herder, 1971.

Ochs, Robert. *The Death in Every Now*. New York: Sheed and Ward, 1969.

Ogden, Schubert. *The Reality of God: And Other Essays*. New York: Harper and Row, 1966.

Otto, Rudolph. *The Idea of the Holy*. Trans by John W. Harvey. New York: Oxford University Press, 1958.

Ramsey, Ian T. *Models and Mystery*. London: Oxford University Press, 1964.

———. *Religious Language: An Empirical Placing of Theological Phrases*. London: SCM Press, 1967.

Ricoeur, Paul. *The Symbolism of Evil*. Trans. by Emerson Buchanan. Boston: Beacon Press Paperback, 1969.

Roberts, Louis. *The Achievement of Karl Rahner*. Foreword by Karl Rahner. New York: Herder and Herder, 1967.

Rogers, Carl. *On Becoming a Person: A Therapist's View of Psychotherapy*. Boston: Houghton Mifflin, 1961.

Röper, Anita. *The Anonymous Christian*. Trans. by Joseph Donceel with an Afterword by Klaus Riesenhuber. New York: Sheed and Ward, 1966.

Rolwing, Richard. "The Idea of Revelation in Karl Rahner." Submitted as a Ph.D. dissertation, University of Iowa, 1975.

Sartre, Jean-Paul. *Being and Nothingness: An Essay on Phenomenological Ontology*. Trans. with an Introduction by Hazel E. Barnes. New York: Washington Square Press, 1966.

Scheler, Max. *On the Eternal in Man*. Trans. by Bernard Noble. Hamden, Conn.: The Shoe String Press, 1972.

Schillebeeckx, E. *God the Future of Man*. Trans. by N. D. Smith. New York: Sheed and Ward, 1968.

Schleiermacher, Friedrich. *On Religion: Speeches to Its Cultured Despisers*. Trans. by John Oman with an Introduction by Rudolf Otto. New York: Harper and Row, 1958.

Shepherd, William C. *Man's Condition: God and the World Process*. New York: Herder and Herder, 1969.

Simons, Eberhard. *Philosophie der Offenbarung: Auseinandersetzung mit Karl Rahner*. Stuttgart: Kohlhammer, 1966.

Skinner, B. F. *Beyond Freedom and Dignity*. New York: Alfred A. Knopf, 1971.

Speck, J. *Karl Rahners theologische Anthropologie, Eine Einführung*. München: Kösel, 1967.

Stohrer, Walter. "The Role of Martin Heidegger's Doctrine of *Dasein* in Karl Rahner's Metaphysics of Man." Ph.D. dissertation, Georgetown University, 1967.

Strawson, P. F. *Individuals: An Essay in Descriptive Metaphysics*. Garden City, N.Y.: Doubleday, 1963.

Tallon, Andrew. "Personization: Person as Personization in Karl Rahner's Philosophical Anthropology." Ph.D. dissertation, Universite Catholique de Louvain, 1969.

Teilhard de Chardin, Pierre. *Human Energy.* Trans. by J. M. Cohen. New York: Harcourt Brace Jovanovich, 1969.

Tillich, Paul. *The Courage To Be.* New Haven, Conn.: Yale University Press, 1952.

————. *Systematic Theology.* 3 vols. combined. Chicago: The University of Chicago Press, 1967.

Tracy, David. *Blessed Rage for Order.* New York: Seabury, 1975; Abbr. *Blessed Rage.*

Tracy, George Edward. "On the Nature of Symbol: As Set Out in the Theology of Karl Rahner." Ph.D. dissertation, Boston College, 1974.

Tyrrell, Francis M. *Man: Believer and Unbeliever.* New York: Alba House, 1974.

van der Heijden, Bert. *Karl Rahner: Darstellung und Kritik seiner Grundpositionen.* Einsiedeln: Johannes, 1973; Abbr. *Darstellung.*

Vorgrimler, Herbert. *Karl Rahner: His Life, Thought and Works.* Trans. by Edward Quinn. Glenn Rock, N.J.: Paulist Press, 1966; Abbr. *Rahner.*

Watts, Alan W. *Psychotherapy East and West.* New York: The New American Library, 1963.

Wess, Paul. *Wie von Gott sprechen? Eine Auseinandersetzung mit Karl Rahner.* Wien: Styria, 1970.

Whitehead, Alfred North. *Process and Reality: An Essay in Cosmology.* New York: The Free Press, 1969.

Wittgenstein, Ludwig. *Tractatus Logico-Philosophicus.* Ed. and trans. by C. K. Ogden and F. P. Ramsey. Introduction by Bertrand Russell. London: Kegan Paul, 1922.

B. Articles

Auer, Johann. "Das Werk Karl Rahners." *Theologische Revue* 60 (1964):145–156.

Baker, Kenneth. "Rahner: The Transcendental Method." *Continuum* 2 (1964):51–59.

Bechtle, Regina. "Karl Rahner's Supernatural Existential: A Personalist Approach." *Thought* 48 (1973):61–77.

Bianchi, Eugene C. "Karl Rahner in New York." *America* 112 (1965):860–863.

Bleistein, Roman. "Mystagogie in den Glauben." *Katholisches Blatt* 1 (1973):30–43.

Bresnahan, James F. "Rahner's Christian Ethics." *America* 123 (1970):351–354.

Brockman, Heinz Wilhelm. "Ein Kursbuch des Glaubens." *Publik-Forum* 18 (September 10, 1976):17–18.

Carmody, John. "Karl Rahner's Brave New Church." *America* 130 (1974):109–111.

———. "Karl Rahner's Theology of the Spiritual Life." *Chicago Studies* 8 (1969):71–86.

———."Rahner's Spiritual Theology." *America* 123 (1970):345–347.

Carr, Anne. "Theology and Experience in the Thought of Karl Rahner." *The Journal of Religion* 13 (1973):359–376.

Clark, Thomas E. "On Americanizing Karl Rahner." *America* 123 (1970):337–339.

Cousins, Ewert. "Models and the Future of Theology." *Continuum* 7 (1969):78–92.

de Vries, J. Besprechung von *Geist in Welt. Scholastik* 15 (1940):404–409.

Donceel, Joseph. "Can We Still Make a Case in Reason for the Existence of God?" In *God Knowable and Unknowable*. Ed. by Robert J. Roth. New York: Fordham University Press, 1973, pp. 159–186.

———. "On Transcendental Thomism." *Continuum* 7 (1969):164–168.

———. "Rahner's Argument for God." *America* 123 (1970):340–342.

———. "Second Thoughts on the Nature of God." *Thought* 46 (1971):346–370.

———. "A Thomistic Misapprehension?" *Thought* 32 (1957):189–198.

Dorcy, Michael M., and Jurich, James P. "A Conversation with Karl Rahner." *America* 120 (1969):733–735.

Dorr, Donal J. "Karl Rahner's 'Formal Existential Ethics.'" *Irish Theological Quarterly* 36 (1969):211–229.

Dulles, Avery. "The Ignatian Experience as Reflected in the Spiritual Theology of Karl Rahner." *Philippine Studies* 13 (1965):471–491.

Dych, William V. "Karl Rahner—An Interview." *America* 123 (1970):356–359.

Eberhard, Kenneth D. "Karl Rahner and the Supernatural Existential." *Thought* 46 (1971):537–561.

———. "Rahner on Religious Education." *Thought* 48 (1973):404–415.

Eicher, Peter, "'Immanenz oder Transzendenz?' Gespräch mit Karl Rahner." *Frieburger Zeitschrift für Philosophie und Theologie* 15 (1968):29–62.

Ernst, Cornelius. Introduction to Rahner's *Theological Investigations*. Vol. 1. Baltimore: Helicon Press, 1961, pp. v–xix.

————. "Some Themes in the Theology of Karl Rahner." *Irish Theological Quarterly* 39 (1965):251–257.

————. "The Theology of Death." *The Clergy Review* 44 (1959):588–602.

Fiorenza, Francis P. "Karl Rahner and the Kantian Problematic." Introduction to Rahner's *Spirit in the World,* 1968, pp. xix–xlv.

Gilkey, Langdon. Review of *Spirit in the World,* by Karl Rahner. *Journal of Ecumenical Studies* 7 (1970):138–144.

Granfield, Patrick. "An Interview: Karl Rahner: Theologian at Work." *American Ecclesiastical Review* 153 (1965):217–230.

Hasenfuss, Josef. Besprechung von *Hörer des Wortes*. *Theologische Revue* 60 (1964):156–157.

Hebblethwaite, Peter. "Karl Rahner's Commitment." *The Month* 231 (1971):136–142.

————. "Relaxing with Karl Rahner." *Commonweal* 101 (1974):111–112.

Hill, William. "Uncreated Grace—A Critique of Karl Rahner." *The Thomist* 27 (1963):333–356.

Kelly, Anthony J. "God: How Near a Relation?" *The Thomist* 34 (1970):191–229.

Kenny, J. Peter. "The Problem of Concupiscence." *Theology Digest* 8 (1960):163–166.

————. "Reflections on Human Nature and the Supernatural." *Theological Studies* 14 (1953):280–287.

Lehmann, Karl. "Karl Rahner." In *Bilanz der Theologie im 20. Jahrhundert IV: Bahnbrechende Theologen.* Ed. by H. Vorgrimler and R. VanderGucht. Frieburg: Herder, 1970, pp. 143–181.

Lindbeck, George A. "The Thought of Karl Rahner, S.J." *Christianity and Crisis* 25 (1965):211–215.

MacKinnon, Edward. "The Transcendental Turn: Necessary But Not Sufficient." *Continuum* 6 (1968):225–231.

Macquarrie, John. "How Is Theology Possible?" *Union Seminary Quarterly* 18 (1963):295–305.

————. "Religous Experience." (Unpublished paper)

————. "Self-Transcending Man." *Commonweal* 91 (1969):155.

Maloney, Donald. "Rahner and the Anonymous Christian." *America* 123 (1970):348–350.

Mann, Peter. "Masters in Israel: IV. The Later Theology of Karl Rahner." *Clergy Review* 54 (1969):936–948.

————. "The Transcendental or the Political Kingdom? I & II." *New Black-friars* 50 (1969):805–812 and 51 (1971):4–16.

Mannermaa, T. "Eine falsche Interpretationstradition von Karl Rahners *Hörer des Wortes?*" *Zeitschrift für katholische Theologie* 92 (1970):204–209.

Masson, Robert. "Rahner and Heidegger: Being, Hearing, and God." *The Thomist* 37 (1973):455–488.

McCool, Gerald A. "The Philosophical Theology of Rahner and Lonergan." In *God Knowable and Unknowable.* Ed. by Robert J. Roth. New York: Fordham University Press, 1973, pp. 123–157.

————. "Philosophy and Christian Wisdom." *Thought* 44 (1969):485–512.

————. "The Philosophy of the Human Person in Karl Rahner's Theology." *Theological Studies* 22 (1961):537–562.

————. "Rahner's Anthropology." *America* 123 (1970):342–344.

Metz, Johannes Baptist. "An Essay on Karl Rahner." Foreword to Rahner's *Spirit in the World,* 1968, pp. xiii–xviii.

————. "Karl Rahner." In *Tendenzen der Theologie im 20. Jahrhundert: Eine Geschichte in Porträts.* Ed. by H. J. Schultz. Stuttgart: Kruez-Verlag, 1966, pp. 513–518.

Moiser, Jeremy. "Why Did the Son of God Become Man?" *The Thomist* 37 (1973):288–305.

Motherway, Thomas J. "Supernatural Existential." *Chicago Studies* 4 (1965):79–103.

Niel, Henri. "Honouring Karl Rahner." *Heythrop Journal* 6 (1965):259–269.

————. "The Old and the New in Theology: Rahner and Lonergan." *Cross Currents* 16 (1966):463–480.

Novak, Michael. "Required: A Concrete Political Starting Place." *Continuum* 6 (1968):235–236.

O'Donoghue, Noel-Dermond. "Rahner: Early Philosophy." *Irish Theological Quarterly* 37 (1970):322–325.

Ogden, Schubert M. "The Challenge to Protestant Thought." *Continuum* 6 (1968):236–240.

————. "The Task of Philosophical Theology." In *The Future of Philosophical Theology.* Ed. by Robert A. Evans. Philadelphia: The Westminster Press, 1971.

O'Meara, Thomas. "Karl Rahner on Priest, Parish, and Deacon." *Worship* 40 (1966):103–110.

Peter, Carl. J. "The Position of Karl Rahner Regarding the Supernatural: A Comparative Study of Nature and Grace." *Proceedings of the Catholic Theological Society of America* 20 (1965):81–94.

Richard, Robert L. "Rahner's Theory of Doctrinal Development." *Proceedings of the Catholic Theological Society of America* 18 (1963):157–189.

Ricoeur, Paul. " 'Response' to Karl Rahner's Lecture: On the Incomprehensibility of God." *The Journal of Religion* 58 (1978 Supplement):126–131.

Riesenhuber, Klaus. "The Anonymous Christian According to Karl Rahner." Afterword to *The Anonymous Christian*, by Anita Roper. New York: Sheed and Ward, 1966, pp. 145–179.

Roberts, Louis. "The Collision of Rahner and Balthasar." *Continuum* 5 (1968):753–757.

Robertson, John C., Jr. "Rahner and Ogden: Man's Knowledge of God." *Harvard Theological Review* 63 (1970):377–407.

Shine, Daniel J. "The Being-Present-To-Itself of Being." *Continuum* 6 (1968):240–245.

Silos, Leonardo R. "A Note on the Notion of 'Selbstvollzug' in Karl Rahner." *Philippine Studies* 13 (1965):461–470.

Surlis, Paul. "Rahner and Lonergan on Method in Theology I & II." *Irish Theological Quarterly* 38 (1971):187–201 and 39 (1972):23–42.

Tallon, Andrew. "Rahner and Personization." *Philosophy Today* 14 (1970):44–56.

———. "Spirit, Freedom, History." *The Thomist* 38 (1974):908–936.

———. "Spirit, Matter, Becoming: Karl Rahner's *Spirit in the World (Geist in Welt)*." *The Modern Schoolman* 48 (1971):151–165.

———. "In Dialog with Karl Rahner: Bibliography of Books, Articles and Selected Reviews, 1939–1978." *Theological Digest* 25 (1978):365–385.

Thompson, William M. "Rahner's Theology of Pluralism." *The Ecumenist* 11 (January–February 1973):17–22.

Tracy, David W. "Why Orthodoxy in a Personalist Age?" *Proceedings of the Catholic Theological Society of America* 25 (1970):78–110.

van Roo, William A. "Reflections on Karl Rahner's 'Kirche und Sakramente'," *Gregorianum* 44 (1963):465–500.

van Voorst, L. Bruce. "Küng and Rahner: Dueling over Infallibility." *The Christian Century* 88 (1971):617–622.

Wallace, William A. "The Existential Ethics of Karl Rahner: A Thomistic Appraisal." *The Thomist* 27 (1963):493–515.

Name Index

Anselm, 107
Aquinas, Thomas, 50, 56, 57,
    134n65

Baillie, John, 128n16
Barth, Karl, 58
Bechtle, Regina, 133n26
Bellah, Robert, 130n4
Berger, Peter, 74, 130n4, 135n6
Bleistein, Roman, 130n5
Blondel, Maurice, 50, 139n29
Bonaventure, 132n11
Branick, Vincent, 118, 129n7
Browarzik, Ulrich, 132n4
Brunner, E., 58
Buber, Martin, 74
Burrell, David, 138n9

Camus, Albert, 7, 141n56
Cirne-Lima, Carlos, 134n61
Cobb, John, 138n7
Coreth, Emerich, 57, 115, 137n11
    13, 138n33 35, 138n6, 139n24
    31 32, 140n54
Cousins, Ewert, 67, 135n8
Cyril of Jerusalem, 127n1

Davies, J. G., 74, 135n6
de Vries, J., 133n38, 140n44
Descartes, René, 50, 57
Donceel, Joseph, 133n38, 134n43,
    139n14 23, 140n40 48 52 54,
    141n58

Duméry, Henry, 74, 135n6,
    137n16, 139n56
Dunne, John, 75, 132n13, 135n6,
    136n22
Dupré, Louis, 135n6

Eberhard, Kenneth D., 133n26
Eicher, Peter, 132n4, 140n44
Ernst, Cornelius, 140n36
Evans, Robert, 135n16

Fiorenza, Francis P., 133n38, 139n33
Fischer, Klaus, 61, 129n26, 131n2,
    134n58, 140n44
Fontinell, Eugene, 139n17 20
Frankl, Viktor, 130n3

Gerken, Alexander, 51, 133n23
Gilkey, Langdon, xiv, 55, 56, 59,
    65, 71, 74, 128n16 17 18,
    130n27, 130n2, 131n14 17 18,
    133n35, 138n5, 141n55
Gilson, Etienne, 56, 134n41
Graham, Aelred, 129n18, 134n62

Heidegger, Martin, 43, 48, 56, 58,
    68, 71, 128n15, 136n4
Heilbroner, Robert, 9
Hepburn, Ronald, 138n4
Hick, John, 141n54
Honecker, Martin, 133n34
Husserl, Edmund, 42, 131n17

161

James, William, 134n59, 135n6
Jaspers, Karl, 129n11
Johann, Robert, 137n27
John, Helen James, 133n39, 139n27

Kant, Immanuel, 50, 56, 57, 110, 112, 113
Keen, Sam, 132n13, 135n6
Kelly, Anthony, 132n4
Kübler-Ross, Elisabeth, 9
Küng, Hans, 59, 74, 107, 131n1

Lonergan, Bernard, 59, 61, 67, 70, 74, 128n18, 129n3, 132n14, 134n41 53 60, 136n22, 136n1 2, 141n54
Lotz, Johannes, 57
Luckmann, Thomas, 130n4

McCool, Gerald, 133n37, 134n46
MacKinnon, Edward, 134n64
Macquarrie, John 58, 66, 68, 74, 128n18, 130n30, 130n7 12, 132n8 14, 135n15, 136n24, 138n36 39, 138n8 11 13, 139n18
Mann, Peter, 133n25
Mannermaa, T. 133n23
Marcel, Gabriel, 137n31
Marcuse, Herbert, 10
Maréchal, Joseph, 48, 50, 56, 57, 112, 139n28 29, 141n54
Maritain, Jacques, 56, 132n4, 133n39, 134n40
Mascall, E. L., 133n38, 141n54
Maslow, Abraham, 129n12, 131n3 8, 136n21
Masson, Robert, 140n44
May, Rollo, 130n3, 137n26
Menninger, Karl, 10
Metz, Johannes, ix, x, 51, 53, 133n25 35
Moiser, Jeremy, 132n4
Moran, Gabriel, 74, 135n6, 136n22, 137n30
Motherhouse, Thomas, 133n26
Muck, Otto, 134n42, 138n6

Newman, John Henry Cardinal, 108
Novak, Michael, 40, 132n13, 135n6, 136n22

O'Donoghue, Noel-Dermond, 140n36
Ogden, Shubert, 51, 70, 74, 127n2, 132n16 18, 132n10, 138n9, 140n36
Origen, 132n11
Ott, Heinrich, 138n9
Otto, Rudolph, 11, 130n7, 135n6

Peter, Carl, 133n26
Plutarch, 127n1

Ramsey, Ian, 68, 73, 132n15, 134n63, 135n7
Ricoeur, Paul, 43, 131n18 19, 134n65
Robertson, John C., 132n12
Robinson, John, 68
Rogers, Carl, 130n3
Roper, Anita, 129n5
Rousselot, P., 50

Sartre, Jean-Paul, 84, 124, 137n25, 141n57
Scheler, Max, 70
Schillebeeckx, E., 74
Schleiermacher, Friedrich, 10, 135n16
Shepherd, William, 54, 133n29
Shine, Daniel J., 140n36
Silos, Leonardo R., 129n2
Simons, Eberhard, 51, 52, 132n23
Skinner, B. F., 137n15 17
Strawson, P. F., 138n8

Tallon, Andrew, 129n2, 140n44
Teilhard de Chardin, Pierre, 59, 137n28

Tillich, Paul, 13, 14, 15, 58, 59, 70,
    73, 74, 128n6 7 8 18, 129n13,
    130n30, 136n24, 136n6
Tracy, David, 66, 74, 128n8 16 18,
    129n10 14 22, 130n1 13,
    131n17, 135n13, 138n5, 140n48
Tyrrel, Francis M., 139n29

van der Heijden, Bert, 131n2
Von Balthasar, Hans Urs, 132n4
Vorgrimler, Herbert, 133n34

Watts, Alan, 129n19, 134n62
Whitehead, Alfred North, 132n6
Wittgenstein, Ludwig, 33, 129n26

Subject Index

Anthropocentric approach, 13, 33, 48, 49, 50, 51, 57, 58, 66

Anthropology: 42, 50, 53, 81, 84; metaphysical, 21, 69, 72, 78, 79, 110

Anxiety, 17, 91, 94

Apologetics: xiii, xiv, 6, 122, 13, 17, 58, 62, 105, 128n2 3; task of, 17, 55, 59, 128n2, 134n65

Apologist, xii, 3–5, 7–11, 16, 18–20, 40, 44, 48, 65, 105, 122, 124

Atheism, 4, 5, 10, 11, 43; atheist, 4, 5, 8, 16, 42, 43; atheistic interpretation, 4, 5, 8, 9, 16

Being: 34, 76, 114, 116, 121, 124, 130n30, 130n7, 139n27, 140n36 44; absolute being, 113, 114, 116, 119, 121

Categorical: 22, 25, 26, 30, 31, 32, 33, 39, 129n4; experience, 23–25; freedom, 86, 140n38; mystagogy, 12, 15, 19, 65, 69; objectification, 27; religious experience, 29–33

Christian doctrine, 12–19

Civilizational malaise, 10

Co-consciousness, 23, 24

Co-knowledge, 24, 60, 108, 114, 120

Computer model, 86, 98

Consciousness, 3, 11, 13, 15–18, 21, 22, 23, 24–26, 39, 42, 45, 56, 61, 62, 69, 70, 76–78, 81, 84, 85, 129n3, 130n7, 131n29

Consciousness raising, 62

Deduction, 121, 139n24

Dynamic spirit, 29, 80, 105

Eclipse of mystery, 5–11, 15, 16, 20, 39, 44, 47, 58, 62, 78, 100

Ecstatic experience, 28, 38, 76

Enlightenment experience, 129n18

Esse: 111–15, 118, 119; absolute, 111, 119; *absolutum,* 119, 120; *commune,* 118, 119

Existence of God: 5, 6, 16, 32, 106, 107, 108, 115–21, 124, 125, 140n40; and the atheist, 7; and human questions, 18; and mystery, 8

Existential: belief, 32; closeness, 37; involvement, 21, 22; phenomenology, 43; question, 14; reality, 32; situation, 29; structure, 101

Existentialism, 7

Experience: finite, 28; lived, 23–27; and Christian doctrine, 12–19, 50, 65; and mystery, 16, 17; of God, 11, 17, 60

Experiential model, 67

Expressive model, 67

Faith, xi, xii, 5, 6, 12, 32, 58, 107, 108, 109, 119, 125

Fides qua, 12

Fides quae, 12

Finite spirit, 25, 49, 60, 82–84, 100, 101, 103, 105, 110

First level of reflection, 108

Freedom: 30, 35, 37, 48, 52, 58, 65, 74, 75, 81, 84–92, 94, 98, 99, 101, 102, 103, 105, 109, 114, 115, 118, 121, 123, 135n6, 137n16 25 27, 138n33; and knowledge, 27, 53; transcendental, 88, 89–91, 101, 102, 140n38

Grace: 14, 15, 31–33, 36, 43, 46, 54, 55, 131n2, 133n28; graced condition, 16; graced matrix, 13; graced self-experience, 46; nature and, 54, 55

Gracious mystery, 7, 19, 35, 37, 38, 42, 45, 50, 65, 69, 88, 92, 93, 95, 97, 98, 105, 106, 109, 114, 115, 116, 125, 126

Humanistic sociology, 40

Humans as symbolic beings, 26

Illative sense, 108

Incarnation, 32, 36

Initiation into mystery, 17–19, 46

Kerygma, 46

Language: of mystery, 5; theological, 41; of transcencence, 5, 9. *See also* Primordial words.

Maieutic, 17

Materiality, 83, 84, 102, 103, 113, 137n13

Metaphysics: 25, 49, 51, 53, 55, 56, 60, 62, 66, 70, 72, 99, 106–10, 121, 125, 132n23; descriptive, 138n8; of knowledge, 56, 57, 60, 70, 113, 114, 134n46

Method of correlation, 13

Models of mystery, 47, 65–74, 75–103

Mystagogical effort: 34, 44; function of theology, 13, 47; models, 68, 69, 71–74, 105; orientation, 46; power, 42; task 13, 18, 22, 48, 59, 62, 69, 75; tool, 45

Mystagogue, 16–19, 27, 39, 40, 42, 43, 44, 104, 128n13

Mystagogy: ix, x, xiv, 7, 11, 12, 16–20, 27, 39, 40, 42, 44, 45–47, 51, 52, 61, 67, 72, 74, 104, 128n2; categorical, 12, 15, 19, 65, 67, 69, 128n2; transcendental, 15–19, 41, 47, 62, 65, 67, 69, 128n18; and self-awareness, 16–19

Mystery: and experience, 7, 8, 36–38; absolute, 27, 29, 46, 50, 51, 73, 84, 89, 91, 97, 101, 103, 107, 108, 116–18, 120, 121; distorted sense of, xviii, 9, 12; holy, 106, 118, 119; and experience, 15–19; and ontologism, 9; and silent believers, 8

Mysticism, 38, 60

Numinous, 11, 130n7, 135n6

Ontological element, 70, 71

Ontological shock, 28

Ontologism, 9, 60, 127n6

Pantheism, 29

Peak experiences, 28, 129n12, 130n8, 136n21

Phenomenological philosophy, 70

Phenomenology: 42, 43, 55, 56, 62, 66, 70–73, 78, 104, 109, 110, 115, 121–23, 135n6, 136n22, 136n2; hermeneutical, 131n18

Pipeline believers, 8, 60, 61

Positivists, 8

Practical theology, 52

Primordial words, 41, 130n9

Privileged experiences, 30

Prolegomenon to theology, xiv, 65, 71

Quasi-formal causality, 140n51

Reduction, 121, 139n24
Reformed subjectivist principle, 132n10
Religious experience, 9, 20–21, 24, 30, 31–33, 36–39, 43, 48, 68, 105, 106, 135n6, 136n22 24
Resurrection, 13, 16
Retorsion, 121, 139n14
Rhapsodic communication, 136n21

Scandal of particularity, 8
Secular: age, xi; culture, 39; humanism, 4; man, 4; people, 58, 65; world, x, 14, 44
Secularism, 127n2
Secularization, 4, 6
Secularized atheist, 4, 5, 43
Secularized consciousness, 6
Self-acceptance, 37, 47, 89, 91–94, 102
Self-actuation, 21, 25, 87, 90, 92, 95, 100, 123
Self-awareness, xiii, 16, 23, 24, 29, 31, 62, 83, 104, 113, 114
Self-confrontation, 44
Self-consciousness, 40
Self-discovery, 73
Self-enactment, 21
Self-experience: i, 19–23, 25, 26, 30, 36, 39, 42–45, 47, 48, 61, 72, 85; and the categorical, 25; and the experience of God, 27, 29, 31, 47; and mystery, 15
Self-fulfillment, 87, 92–93, 95
Self-interpretation, 5, 19, 23, 24, 39, 43
Self-knowledge, 20, 23
Self-modification, 49
Self-possession, 24, 51, 82–84, 94, 101, 102
Self-presence, 49, 79, 82–84, 94, 103, 113, 114, 140n36

Self-realization, 26, 29, 30, 35, 79
Self-reflection, 18, 77
Self-transcendence, 35, 47, 76, 114
Self-understanding, 3, 4, 13, 16, 18, 22, 39, 43, 72, 100, 101, 108, 122, 123, 136n22
Silent believers, 8, 33
Sisyphian heroes, 7, 124
Skeptical attitude, 11
Skeptics, 6, 7, 124, 125, 141n59 60
Spirit, 10, 25, 28, 49, 59, 79–84, 100, 103, 105, 107, 111, 114
Spiritual activity, 34
Spiritual depth psychology, 17, 24
Spiritual dynamism, 28, 29, 35, 37, 38, 62, 82, 99, 110, 118
Spiritual striving, 118
Symbols, 26, 42, 70, 72, 122, 131n18, 132n23, 136n22

Theological circle, 14
Theology: 3, 12–14, 31, 33, 43, 45–54, 57–61, 65, 66, 73, 107, 128n10, 134n46, 141n55; anthropocentric, 13, 50, 57
Third force in psychology, 39
Transcendent goal, 6, 33–36, 38
Transcendental: awareness, 24–26, 29, 62; deduction, 139n25; experience, 23, 24, 27, 30, 31, 37, 38, 131n28; method, 69, 78, 106–108, 111, 121, 138n6; mystagogy, 15–19, 41, 47, 62, 65, 67, 128n18; and categorical, 23, 26, 31, 33, 38, 52, 61
Transcendentality: 28–30, 34–36, 42, 53, 62, 69, 73, 83, 102; human transcendence, 28, 33, 35, 37, 38, 46, 47, 53, 59, 60, 100, 101, 103, 105, 106, 110, 111, 115–21

Wooing of an elite, 43, 44